THE WHOLE STORY

Natural Learning and the Acquisition of Literacy in the Classroom

BRIAN CAMBOURNE

Ashton Scholastic

Auckland   Sydney   New York   Toronto   London

Edited by Libby Handy and Penny Scown
Designed by Alan Harris
Photographs by Jan Turbill

First published 1988

Ashton Scholastic Limited
Private Bag 1, Penrose, Auckland 6, New Zealand.

Ashton Scholastic Pty Ltd
PO Box 579, Gosford, NSW 2250, Australia.

Scholastic Inc.
730 Broadway, New York, NY 10003, USA.

Scholastic-TAB Publications Ltd
123 Newkirk Road, Richmond Hill, Ontario L4C 3G5, Canada.

Scholastic Publications Ltd
Marlborough House, Holly Walk, Leamington Spa, Warwickshire CV32 4LS, England.

National Library of New Zealand
Cataloguing-in-Publication data

CAMBOURNE, Brian
    The whole story : natural learning and the
acquisition of literacy in the classroom / by
Brian Cambourne ; (edited by Libby Handy and
Penny Scown), — Auckland, N.Z. : Ashton Scholastic,
1988. — 1 v.
    ISBN 0-908643-49-7
            372.414
    1. Reading (Elementary) — Language experience
approach.   2.   English language — Study and teaching
(Elementary).   I.   Handy, Libby, 1941-   II.   Scown,
Penny.   III.   Title.

54321   89/8 012/9

Typeset in Garamond by Rennies Illustrations, Auckland NZ
Printed in Singapore by Singapore National Printers Ltd

Contents

The English language has many perplexing features, not the least of which is the absence of a non-discriminatory pronoun. The writer in this instance has opted for the established convention — although not without some misgivings!

1

What it's All About

This is a book about one of the most magnificent of human achievements — the remarkable ability of the human mind to create meaning using patterns of squiggly marks which can be recorded on paper or some other material. Essentially, it is a book about children learning to read and write. Because of this it must also be a book about teachers teaching children to read and write.

In this book I present a very personal view of how I think teachers should go about helping learners become what I call 'successful' readers/writers. Successful readers/writers have at least four things in common. **Firstly**, they are confident readers and writers — reading and writing tasks rarely intimidate them. **Secondly,** they display high degrees of control over the processes which underpin reading and writing. **Thirdly**, while they appreciate the communicative functions which reading and writing serve, they also know how to use reading and writing as media for enhancing thinking and learning. **Fourthly**, they continue to engage in and enjoy reading and writing long after formal instruction has ceased. While I refer to this as a personal view, it is also a theory of literacy education which has now been evolving for about a decade.

It is not an 'off the cuff' or 'top of the head' or 'armchair' theory, nor, I hope, is it an esoteric, 'ivory tower, airy-fairy, impractical' theory. It has evolved as a consequence of hundreds of hours of both observing and participating with learners engaged in using and learning language in the classroom, playground and home settings. It is also the result of endless hours spent in interviewing teachers, children and parents about learning and about reading and writing. It could be said that for the last decade I've been engaged in a kind of educational anthropology, trying to make sense out of the ways that learning and literacy come together in various settings. In the jargon of educational research it would be labelled a 'grounded theory'. This means that the theoretical principles which emerge can be traced back to the observations and data in which they were originally 'grounded'. The result is a theory of literacy learning which is grounded in the real world of learning as it occurs in real classrooms. Hopefully, it is also a practical theory which teachers will be able to use.

Inevitably, such a theory will have implications for teaching as well. The theory which I present in this book is no exception in that many who read it will find that it raises questions about (and in some instances rejects) many of the long-held, traditional beliefs about how reading and writing should be learned and taught. Because of this it may disturb or even offend some readers. Nevertheless, it is an honest attempt to explain why I think some approaches to literacy education can be detrimental to learners. Finally, it will offer some advice on what can be done to make the teaching of reading and writing more theoretically valid.

It is only fair to bring out into the open some beliefs and prejudices which I hold about literacy. The beliefs are related to how I think about literacy. The prejudices relate to how I think literacy should be taught.

My Personal Beliefs about Literacy

The term 'literacy' means different things to different people and different cultures. Over two hundred years ago in England literacy was equated with classical knowledge, i.e. knowledge of Greek and Latin. In the early days of convict settlement in Australia, convicts were classified as literate if they could write their names and read some verses from the Bible. In some Middle Eastern countries, literacy is equated with the attainment of four years of schooling. More recently, the notion of a 'basic' or 'functional' literacy tied to the everyday needs of society has emerged. The more one reads into the historical and demographic literature on literacy, the more obvious it becomes that literacy is a relative term, and that what it actually means will vary as the values of any culture vary. Currently, the view in our culture and in other similar western cultures, seems to equate literacy with scores on standardised tests of reading and spelling.

My views on what literacy is (and is not) are different from the prevailing view. Firstly, in my view, literacy is not a single entity or definite physical reality like the amount of water in a container or the amount of gas in a cylinder. Nor is it a single ability or skill like typing or using a calculator. To think of literacy in this way is to fall into the logical trap of reification, i.e. fallaciously referring to something which is complex and abstract as if it were 'thing-like' and concrete. The history of psychology is strewn with such fallacies of misplaced concreteness; intelligence, aggression, motivation, anxiety and learning, to name but a few.

One of the dangerous consequences of using terms which reify is that soon one starts acting towards them as if they do acutally represent concrete, tangible entities. I suppose the best exemplar of this is the widespread belief that concepts like literacy, intelligence, motivation, aggression and anxiety can actually be measured and quantified as if they were analogous to something like the amount of oxygen in a room.

To me, literacy is a word which describes a whole collection of behaviours, skills, knowledge, processes and attitudes. It has something to do with our ability to use language in our negotiations with the world. Often these negotiations are motivated by our desires to manipulate the world for our own benefit. Reading and writing are two linguistic ways of conducting these negotiations. So are talking, listening, thinking, reflecting, and a host of other behaviours related to cognition and critical thinking.

I happen to believe that in our culture these negotiations are enhanced and extended if we have acquired control of as wide a range of language forms as possible. The more language forms we have internalised and can use appropriately, the more successful our negotiations with our world will be. This is another way of saying that the more control we have over language forms and the more we use them and refine them, the more we are empowered.

This is especially true of the academic literacy which schools set out to develop. The linguistic registers (ways of organising and putting discourse together) which are characteristically associated with different academic disciplines are the basis of thinking and knowing and, ultimately, of learning, in these disciplines. The more of these registers we acquire and use, the better our ability to think and learn in these fields. Sustained engagement with these forms increases the probability that they will be ultimately internalised and brought under control. Sustained reading and writing with different textual forms are probably two of the most effective ways possible of internalising and, ultimately, controlling these forms.

To me, literacy culminates in the active, critical, productive thinking and problem solving that results from control of those language forms and control of those language processes which make it possible for us to successfully negotiate both our school (academic) world and the world outside school. To me, literacy manifests itself in sustained reading, writing, talking, listening, thinking, remembering, selecting, organising, inferencing, and other cognitive behaviours.

Some Prejudices: Read these First!

Although I call them 'prejudices', I do so reluctantly. To me they are more accurately described as *axioms*, i.e. self-evident truths. All this means is that I can't 'prove' them in the empirical sense, (I doubt if anyone could), but I would find it difficult to believe that anyone could seriously disagree with them. Because they are axiomatic for me, I assume that they are equally axiomatic for others. Let me state them in point form:

1) Learning to read, write, spell, punctuate, etc., (i.e., learning to become literate) ought to be as uncomplicated and barrier-free as possible.
2) Once learned, the skills and knowledge that make literacy possible ought to endure beyond the four walls of the classroom; that is, they should be 'durable'.

Let me elaborate on each:

Learning to become literate ought to be as uncomplicated and barrier-free as possible.

When I argue that learning to be literate ought to be as uncomplicated and barrier-free as possible, I'm definitely not advocating challenge-free, 'funsy-wunsy' learning which is stripped of the need for what many teachers refer to as **effort** or **challenge**. On the contrary. When I state this position I do not mean that learners should expect to learn without experiencing puzzlement or cognitive unrest — even frustration — or to avoid what I've referred to as the **privilege of struggling**. Rather I mean that artificial barriers which unnecessarily complicate the learning process, or which serve only to confuse learners, have no place in the process of learning to become literate. I believe that there is a difference between **struggling** to learn or find the solution to a problem and **suffering** while you try to solve it. Struggle is an essential part of all learning. Any pleasure that comes from learning is associated with it. Somehow we feel a little nobler when we master something after struggling with it.

I think it's got something to do with what craftsmen and poets have called 'the joy of achievement'. This is what partly explains why young children will lie in bed at night practising the language forms which they're trying to get under control. This is why I think computer afficionados will spend endless hours trying to write complex programmes just to see them run. This is why I think professional authors persevere with their writing even though they will readily tell you that writing is not easy, nor is it comfortable or enjoyable.

It seems that any learning associated with creating meaning through any medium typically involves some kind of struggle before the full potential of that medium is under control — art, music and mime, as well as print. Furthermore, there appears to be something genuinely pleasurable derived from the struggle which is experienced in these situations. Remove the struggle and you remove the pleasure. Turn the struggle into suffering and you achieve the same end — unpleasant or joyless learning. Perhaps this 'struggle/pleasure' relationship has something to do with the brain's apparent **need** to be continually constructing meaning, to be continually imposing sense and order on chaos. When the brain is successful in making sense and/or imposing order, it's a little like feeding a hungry organism its favourite food — satisfaction follows. Later I shall argue that some approaches, rather than minimise complexity, maximise the probability that boredom, confusion, 'non-sense', and therefore joyless and ineffective learning, will occur.

Once learned, the skills of literacy should be durable.

By this I mean that children should find that the end result of the struggle which they experience when engaged in learning to read and write has been so worthwhile that they will continue to use what they've learned outside the four walls of their classrooms and for the rest of their lives.

By this I mean that having learned to read, learners will continue, long after formal instruction has ceased, to turn to books and other kinds of texts for information, for pleasure, for escape or for learning.

By this I mean that having learned to write they will continue to use writing to help them identify and solve problems, to help them clarify their thinking, to help them learn, as well as to help them communicate with others.

Everything I advocate in this book is related to these two axioms (prejudices?) and the corollaries which flow from them. If you vehemently disagree with them you may find the rest of the book annoying and possibly offensive. If you agree with them you may find the book satisfying and useful.

5

2

Portraits of Literacy Learning

In the kind of research I do, it is necessary to rewrite the shorthand notes I take during interviews and reflect upon them. These reflections typically become 'summary stories' of what the interviews revealed. Here is the summary story I wrote after interviewing a Grade 5 boy named Glen.

Portrait No. 1: The Case of Glen

Glen is just over ten years of age and in Grade 5 at primary school. I've been talking with him for just over an hour. In the course of our conversation I've asked him to tell me about the books he's read, how he reads, how he handles fictional and expository text, how he chooses a book, what he does when he's blocked by text which he finds difficult, how he writes, when he writes, and generally how he gets through the language activities of the day in his classroom.

I am impressed by the maturity of the responses he makes to my probes. Glen displays a great deal of explicit, specialist knowledge about a wide variety of aspects of his own literacy behaviour. I am even more impressed by the range of books he's read. He's an expert on Roald Dahl, Beverly Cleary and Colin Thiele; he discusses plot structure and the problems faced by each as an author; he thinks the best piece of writing he's ever read is the first two paragraphs of Chapter 3 of *Charlotte's Web* in which E.B. White describes a barn. He says it's 'good writing' because White describes the feelings and sights and smells and sounds 'as if he's really been in a barn and paid attention to all the details while he was there'. Glen explains to me how to use an encyclopaedia, atlas, thesaurus and dictionary and demonstrates with examples, 'just in case I didn't catch on'. He explains how reading to find information is different from reading to 'get into the story', and uses the term 'skim reading' in his explanation. When I ask how he's learned so much in such a short time he pauses for a moment then says, 'I guess I just listen to other kids and I watch how they do things. Sometimes I talk with the teacher; often I just have a go and share my attempt with someone who can help me. If I get stuck I find somebody who can give me advice. In this class you can always put hard things away and come back to them later when you learn a bit more about how it's done.'

Glen's reading log shows that over the last third of the year he has finished ten works of fiction and two non fiction. The average length of each is 112 pages. He has learned by heart a poem of at least twenty lines. His writing log shows he has completed three fictional pieces and two expository pieces. A check of these 'public' pieces reveals an almost perfect proofreading of spelling has taken place. His writing folder is filled with unfinished pieces of writing which he 'might come back and work on later'. He is currently working his way through C.S. Lewis's *Voyage of the Dawntreader* and is waiting for the class copy of *The Lion, the Witch and the Wardrobe* to become free because he's 'starting to find fantasy interesting'.

Is Glen one of those precocious fifth grade 'bookworm' kids that pop up in the odd class now and then? A look at his educational history reveals that nothing could be further from the truth. He had been classified as 'severely learning disabled' two years prior and had spent the last two years in a remedial class. He had all the classic symptoms of what Special Educators label 'Specific Learning Disability'. His verbal I.Q. was too low to assess, but his non-verbal I.Q. was one standard deviation above the norm. At the beginning of the school year he scored in the bottom stanine, i.e. bottom 4% of population, on a standardised test of reading which emphasised comprehension. His score on a standardised test of spelling also placed him in the bottom stanine. His previous teachers had described him as 'showing severe retardation in all aspects of literacy'. His mother described him as a non-reader and non-speller.

Eight months later, he and his whole class were re-tested using parallel forms of the same instruments. Glen's results put him in the fifth stanine for both reading and spelling, but it was obvious from my interview that he was an avid, competent, confident reader and writer, and an average speller. While Glen had made remarkable progress both in the standardised tests and in terms of what he'd read and produced as a writer, and what he knew about the processes, his performance was not exceptional when compared with his class peers. Rather, by comparison with them, he was still, according to his teacher, 'average'. Although he'd not been singled out for any special remedial treatment in the traditional sense, Glen had made significant gains in a wide range of literacy-related learnings.

Portrait No. 2: The Case of Ivanka

As well as interviewing learners, I've also spent a great deal of time observing them and trying to capture in written form what I observe. In the jargon of educational research, these written observations are called 'specimen records'. Here are some specimen records which I took while observing Ivanka. At the time of writing this book she was beginning her third year of school. The records below describe her first days at school and then what she was doing about one year later. She was one of a group of Macedonian children who could neither speak nor comprehend spoken English when they began formal schooling. The field notes I wrote as I observed Ivanka on that first day of school are as follows:

Day 1: Ivanka sits near Blaguna. She is very tearful. The bilingual teacher speaks to her in Macedonian but it doesn't seem to help very much. Ivanka observes what the other children are doing, picks up her pencil and paper and through tear-filled eyes begins to put marks on the paper. As I lean over to get a closer look, her crying becomes more intense but I can make out that she appears to be writing her name using what looks like lower case alphabetic script. (Or is it Cyrillic? I need to check this out with the bilingual aide.) She keeps looking at the name label which the teacher has pinned to her blouse. She is, I suspect, copying her name. She displays good control over the pencil; she has obviously used one before. Whether she realises that the label represents her name or not is uncertain. The fact that she's omitted the letter 'k' and the horizontal lines from the top and bottom of the vertical stroke of the capital 'I' suggests that she's not copying slavishly, although she is so tearful that it is doubtful she can see much at all.

(Subsequent discussion with the bilingual teacher suggested that Ivanka knew that the label represented her name.)

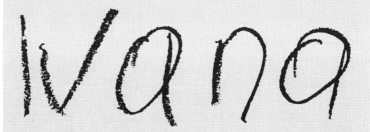

About One Year Later

Ivanka brings this piece of writing to her teacher:

First attempt 28/3

The frog is just

jumping and the

frog is slide

in to water

then the frog

is find a spider

and the frog

is eat the

spider

The FroKo is Iv.ahka jasa jaPinK FoKoa and The is SLEcs in to woata then The Frak is Fain a spaDa and The Farkc is iteiae the spaDa

and the

frog is just

jumping in the

in water is

jump tree

and frog is

find another

spider and

the frog is eat spider

aned ITthe FroKae is jast japiK inThe FrinWotae is Jaite trie and Froka is Faitn a naD spiDa and ite The FrKoa is sai

Here is the summary story I wrote at the time of reviewing Ivanka's development over a year.

10

She read the Frog/Spider piece in English. It represents her written retelling of a story which the teacher has read to the class. Ivanka has obviously engaged with the story for she chose to produce another version of it the next day, and a different version again about a week later. A comparison of her repeated attempts reveals some remarkable learning has been going on, especially with respect to English spelling.

Second attempt 9/4

The frog is
jumping in to
water and the
frog is find
a spider and
the frog is
eat the
spider an the
frog is happy

Ivanku   9/9/84
The Frog is
japK IN +o
wo+a and The
Frog is FAIvon
a spaiDa and
The Frog is
eiD+a The
spaiDa and The
Frog is Hepi

and the friend
is come and
the friend said
Hello frog and
the frog said
Hello my friend
and the frog
is sleeping and
the frog is find
another spider and
the frog is eat
the spider

and The Frece
is Kamma and
The Frece and
sete
HaLo Frog and
The Frog sete
HoLo my
Frece
and The Frog
is slipmk and
The Frog
a NaDa saiDa Fair
The Frog is etet
The spaDa is etet

11

In her first text (28/3), Ivanka spelled the same words differently on a number of occasions. For example:

Frog = Froko, Fokoa, Frako, Farko, Frokae, Froka, Frkoa

spider = SpaDa, spaDa, Spida, sais

find = Fain, Faitn

eat = ite, ite, iae

jumping = japink, jaite

However, her second text shows a much greater consistency of spelling and, in the majority of cases, the words more closely resemble conventional spelling, e.g.

frog = Frog, Frog, Frog, Frog, Frog, etc.

spider = spaiDa, spaiDa, SpaiDa

find = fain, Fain

eat = eiDta, etet

jumping = japk

10/4

Ivanka's English has improved so much that she can now hear the segments of sound within words, as her attempts at representing English show. She can demonstrate to other children how she does this, meticulously isolating the sound segments in English words and finding the graphic equivalents on the alphabet chart. She has become so proficient at this that she is the acknowledged 'resource person' for helping her peers with a phonemic segmentation spelling strategy. She is reading many of the same books that other, native-born English-speaking children in Grade 1 are reading. Furthermore, she has a few favourites which are well above what most teachers would judge to be of Grade 1 level. She can read these aloud. When asked to do so, the miscues which she makes indicate that she is focused on meaning but has some problems with English grammar. (These problems are diminishing.) What is more important is that she no longer cries. She will tell adults (such as researchers who sit in her classroom) that she likes reading and writing in English, and that she thinks she is getting better at it.

It is significant that Ivanka has not had any formal or direct instruction in traditional phonics, nor has she had any traditional spelling instruction. Because of the lack of resources in the school she has not learned to read or write in her first language, although she had indicated during interviews that her mother sometimes gets her to do some 'Macedonian ABC' practice at home. Ivanka is not a special case. The majority of her class group has made similar kinds of gains in the spoken and written control of English.

Portrait No. 3: The Case of Nicole

At the time that I was observing her, Nicole was a pert, pretty, precocious (in the nice sense), pigtailed blonde, aged five years three months. Her first language was English. She was the first of two children of professional, middle-class parents. The date was 11 November when she began working on a piece of writing that was to keep her occupied for up to forty minutes a day for a full month. It ran to twenty-seven pages and was still unfinished on 12 December when I collected it.

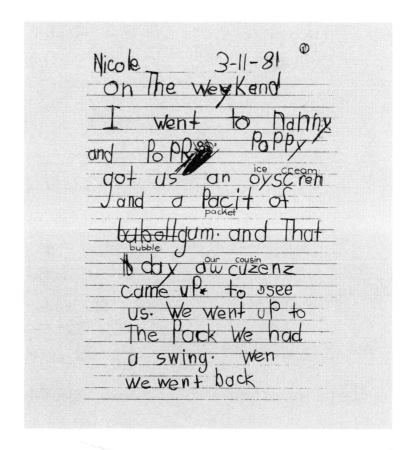

We Went to see
aw dnty Melt
at The covent.
aw cusenz &
fownd a Pond.
thein Was a fish
in the water.
aw cuzens fownd
a Plastic bag.

Ma th you
trid to cach him.
and scot took his
thongs off. and
hoPed in the Pond.
and trid to cach
the fish. I luft
and luft. & Scot
looked So fony.
We wanted a ball

Some Reflections on Nicole's Development

The following are the reflective notes which I made on Nicole's development when the project in which she was a subject was drawing to a close. The 'it' refers to the twenty-seven page epic that Nicole wrote:

10/12/81

Though not a literary masterpiece (it conforms to what Donald Graves has labelled a 'bedtime to bedtime story'), it does reveal a remarkable degree of control over many of the conventions of written English. My earlier field notes show that Nicole was a hard subject to observe for she did all of her processing covertly, simply staring into space and then putting pencil to paper. In order to find out what was going on inside her head I had to probe relentlessly during the many open-ended interviews I had with her. The results of these probing sessions revealed that Nicole read avidly and paid very close attention to how words looked, 'because one day I might want to use them in my writing'. Nicole was one of a group of seventy plus kindergarten (new entrant) children who had entered school some eight months previously. Like the majority of this group she was then a non-reader and non-writer. At the end of the school year the scores on standardised tests of literacy that the principal of the school had given every new entrant class for the previous six years showed that Nicole's cohort had scored at levels which were significantly higher than those which had passed through the school previously.

So What?
What Do these Portraits Tell Us?

What is the point or significance of these portraits? Are they merely a collection of cute success stories? If so, so what? In every large school system there will be those unique teachers who seem to work miracles with a wide range of children. All that these portraits **prove** is that talented teachers are found all over the world — even in the Antipodes.

Now, while it is true that talented teachers who can work miracles may be found all over the world, what is special about the teachers who taught Glen, Ivanka and Nicole is that they each had made quite dramatic and significant changes in the ways that they thought about, and therefore taught, literacy. None of them would have described themselves as 'specially talented'. All regarded themselves as competent, average kinds of practitioners. They did, however, have three things in common:

Firstly, each of them had expressed a strong sense of frustration and dissatisfaction with the ways that they had been teaching the skills of literacy to the children in their classes.

Secondly, as a consequence of this frustration and dissatisfaction, each of them realised that they were tied to a model of learning which was not only out of date but which was based on quite dubious assumptions. Furthermore, they each came to the conclusion that they were (metaphorically) prisoners of a model of learning which locked them into ways of teaching that made learning complex, dysfunctional and trivial.

Thirdly, they tried to break free from the model which had imprisoned them and which had stunted and trivialised their teaching, by developing and implementing a different model of learning based on the remarkable human capacity to learn language **naturally**.

This book is about the model of learning that these teachers implemented. The intention is to give other teachers who may be similarly dissatisfied and/or frustrated with the methods that they're using to teach literacy, the understanding and knowledge that will enable them not only to evaluate what they do in the name of literacy education but, if necessary, help them change. I shall argue that one of the reasons for the dissatisfaction and frustration which teachers experience is that they are prisoners of a model of learning, which, although based on quite invalid assumptions, is not only still taught in our teacher training institutions but has very strong support among the general population as well. In this sense, this book is fundamentally about liberating teachers from that model of learning so that children, in turn, can become liberated learners.

3

Prisoners of
a Model of Learning?

What Does this Mean?

What do I mean when I state that 'teachers are prisoners of a model of learning'? Simply this: what teachers actually **do** when engaged in the act of teaching is motivated by what they **believe** about learners and what they **believe** about the processes which underlie learning. Like most human activity, teaching behaviour is not a random sequence of haphazard events. Teachers plan the lessons they give, buy the materials they use, allocate the time they have, say the things they say, treat children the way they do, evaluate the way they evaluate, reward and punish the way they do, and so on, because of what they believe about the way learning occurs and how it can be brought about. I regard this set of beliefs about learning as a 'theory' or a 'model' which each teacher carries around inside her head.

My thesis is quite simple: the majority of teachers have accepted, unquestioningly, a set of beliefs about learning which had its origins in what Arthur Koestler once called 'the dark ages of psychology' *(Koestler 1975)*, and while they continue to hold these beliefs, they will continue to organise their teaching behaviour in ways which reflect them. True, they may from time to time purchase a new reading scheme which they will assert is 'different' or they may buy a new

17

spelling laboratory or writing kit, but the way they use these materials will not really be very different from the way in which they used the schemes, laboratories and kits which preceded them. Just as prisoners are locked into a context which permits a very limited range of behavioural options, so they are locked into a range of teaching behaviours which, while they may vary in **emphasis** from time to time, will not vary in **substance**.

One could argue that a set of **beliefs** is not the same as a **theory**. I have no qualms about equating the two. True, most teachers would not admit to being **theoretical** (they equate theory with an airy-fairy lack of practical relevance), nor would they be able to state their beliefs about learning and teaching in elegant theoretical terms of the kind found in learned academic journals. Nevertheless, if one regards a theory as a device for explaining why a certain sequence of events occurs, then **beliefs** and other kinds of intuitive know-how can be legitimately accorded the status of **theory**. Every teacher I've ever asked — and in the course of my research I've asked many — can tell me why they teach the way they do. Some are a little more eloquent than others but so far all have been capable of offering an explanation and/or justification of what they do in their classrooms. In other words, teachers can tell others what **theory** guides their teaching behaviour. The difference between saying, 'I **believe** that literacy should be taught this way . . .' and 'My **theoretical** orientation is . . .' to me seems trivial.

The Chains that Bind:
the Model of Learning which Guides Most Teachers

What is this theory or model of learning which has imprisoned the majority of teachers?

Reduced to its simplest terms, it is something like this:

Learning is essentially habit formation. Effective learning is the establishment of 'good' or 'desirable' habits and the prevention of and/or elimination of 'bad' or 'undesirable' habits. Habits are formed through association between stimuli and responses. The degree to which something is learned is a function of the strength of the association between stimulus and response. Repetition strengthens the associative bond between stimulus and response.

During the 1940s and 1950s when this theory was most popular it was not difficult to apply its principles to the learning of language, especially the written forms of language. When viewed from the perspective of **habit formation**, learning to read, write, spell, punctuate, and so on, becomes a process of identifying those habits which need to be formed, breaking them down into subsets and/or hierarchies of stimuli and responses, and then ensuring that they are optimally associated. It is a very mechanistic view of learning which lends itself to the notion of teaching as a kind of 'scientific cognitive engineering' with teachers as controllers of the process. Errors take on a special significance when learning is viewed from this perspective. Errors are **wrong patterns** which, if left untreated, are the beginnings of bad habits. Therefore, before an error, i.e. a potential habit, becomes too strongly established it must be eradicated. Thus, one side of the learning coin becomes a process of constantly practising the right patterns until they become habitual and automatic. The other side is the avoidance and ruthless eradication of wrong forms before they have a chance of becoming fixed. I am prepared to argue that many common classroom practices have their roots in this view of learning.

An Example of the Habit-Formation View of Learning, in Practice

Perhaps the simplest, most clear-cut example of this model of learning in practice is the way that spelling is taught by the majority of teachers in this country. Although the peripheral details may vary from teacher to teacher, when most spelling programmes are reduced to their core elements there is a depressing sameness about them.

The core elements, with minor variations, are as follows:

Children have to be coerced into rote memorising the spelling of preselected lists of words. Rote memorisation, i.e. habit formation, is based on repetition, i.e. associative strength. Therefore, spelling is best taught by insisting that children carry out as many repetitions of the correct form of the chosen words as possible.

In the research that I've been doing in the last ten years, I've witnessed some clever and exciting teaching strategies which teachers have designed in response to these principles. In Australia it is usually called 'drill' It is perceived by both teachers and children to be 'work'. One metaphor which a teacher used as we walked back to the staffroom after he'd shown me how he thought such lessons ought to be taught succinctly summarised this perception. He asked, 'Did you like that lesson, Brian?' Before I could respond, he continued, 'I thought it went rather well. I really **pounded** the words into their heads today, didn't I?' The metaphor conjures up an image of a group of reluctant, empty vessels being forcibly filled with a predetermined number of litres of spelling fact.

The other side of the spelling equation is that these same children should never be exposed to an error of spelling. Teachers are considered less than professional and their competency is usually questioned if they either misspell a word on the chalkboard or wall chart, or miss the opportunity to root out an error in a child's book. The time and effort that teachers are expected to put into marking books is one of the most common complaints that they make about their jobs. When one examines how teachers mark books and asks them why they go about it in the ways that they do, one thing becomes obvious — book marking is essentially an exercise in error identification. While spelling errors have the highest priority, punctuation and grammatical errors aren't far behind. When I probe a little and ask teachers why they have this almost Messianic zeal about the identification of errors in children's books, the typical response is a puzzled expression (What a stupid question!), accompanied by an exasperated, 'So they won't learn them (the errors), of course!'

There's a rather sad paradox here: teachers and children have to **work** really hard to learn the correct forms (pound them into the kids' heads) but the wrong form, if incidentally glimpsed on a chalkboard, chart or if left in a book for a child to see, will, with minimal effort on the learner's part, become permanently fixed in his repertoire of spellings. It's what I've called 'the original sin, children are inherently evil' theory of learning to spell.

Is this Habit-Formation View of Learning Applied to Other Subject Areas?

While the example of the teaching of spelling given above seems to encapsulate most of the principles of the habit-formation theory of learning, traces of it can be found in the methods used in many of the other so-called language arts. Most of us learned to read in classrooms where errors were forbidden, even if meaning was maintained, and which included endless practice (repetition) of carefully worked out sequences of sub-skills in order to make the good habit a permanent, fixed part of our repertoire of responses. Most of us can probably remember writing lessons which consisted of attempts to produce error-free, one-draft texts on topics chosen for us by the teacher or from the textbook she was using. Our texts were collected, corrected and all our errors drawn to our attention. We then learned the correct response (habit) through rewriting the correct forms over and over again (association through repetition).

Grammar, punctuation, literature and the other accoutrements of literacy were taught according to similar principles. Although the specific details of the many lessons given each week, month and year by teachers would vary from teacher to teacher and from language arts lesson to language arts lesson, the general plan which lay behind most of these lessons had its origins in this habit-formation view of the learning process.

The Typical Habit-Formation Lesson Plan

The plan went something like this — first the total literacy act was fragmented into subsets of logically determined and sequenced **concepts** or **skills**. This was typically done by 'experts' who worked outside of classrooms and wrote textbooks for teachers. One or several of these fragments of literacy were then presented to the whole class, usually by means of verbal explanation by the teacher. The flow of information was predominantly one way (teacher to children) but the occasional question on the content of the teacher's discourse was asked to allow for pupil participation. At the conclusion of the verbal explanation of the concept or skill, the children were expected to apply the knowledge, usually in the form of a written exercise of some sort. The basis of most of these written exercises was repetition of the concept/skill which had been explained. The written exercises were typically based on contrived examples. These written responses were typically used by the teacher to make decisions about the success or failure of various pupils in their mastery of the particular sub-skill or sub-concept being taught. This process was repeated day after day until sufficient of the sub-skills and sub-concepts had been mastered and the total act, which was fragmented, was supposed to come together in the learners' heads.

It is my opinion, based on a decade or more of observing teachers in action, talking with them both formally and informally, examining their preparation and evaluation procedures, listening to and analysing the questions which they ask about teaching and learning (especially questions which relate to literacy education), that the general plan which underpinned most of the school learning that my generation experienced is still very popular with today's teachers — and parents! In short, not much change has taken place with respect to the basic theory on which the majority of teachers base their teaching behaviour. Scratch most of today's teachers and parents and you'll find a 'learning-as-habit-formation' theorist lurking just below the surface.

So What?
What's So Wrong with this View of Learning?

You may well ask, 'So what? The majority of us have learned to read, haven't we? Furthermore, there are more and more students staying on at school for the maximum period possible, aren't there? More students than ever before are presenting themselves for admission to universities and other institutions of higher learning. Despite the mechanistic ways in which they were taught, something must have been right with the model of learning which was used by these students' teachers, mustn't it?'

Such comments seem to make sound common sense. Like most common sense notions, however, they conceal as much as they reveal. While it is true that levels of **literacy** (whatever that term means!) have risen among the general population in the last quarter century, when examined closely, literacy usually means **reading**. Furthermore, when one looks at the evidence, it seems to fall into one of three main categories.

(1) Demographic surveys over time of trends revealed by standardised tests.
(2) Trends in the publishing trade — more books and magazines than ever before per head of population.
(3) The assertion that there has been an increase in both the amount and the complexity of the material with which readers are expected to cope.

While I have no reason to doubt the truth of these data (although some of the raw figures in the original studies have often been difficult and sometimes impossible to understand), they only present part of the picture. There are other facets of the total picture which data such as these do not reveal. Let me share some of these other facets.

Habit-Formation Learning
and the Teaching of Reading

Over the last decade I've kept accurate records of the requests made by worried parents and concerned teachers to the institutions at which I've been employed. I am concerned at the increase in requests for help for young learners which usually begin like this:

Dr Cambourne, I've got this child who can read but who never seems to pick up a book or magazine or newspaper or even a comic. He can get a reasonable score on the tests he's given and if I really force him to read something he can read it, but unless I constantly nag him or force him, he would never engage with even the simplest of texts. What can I do?

Charlotte Huck referred to this type of child over a decade ago as the 'illiterate literate, the child who can read but prefers not to'. My records, which show a significant increase in requests for help for this kind of learner, have been recently confirmed by some survey research on a nationwide sample of Australian students from both primary and secondary levels of the school spectrum *(Bunbury, 1985)*. This study was subtitled, **Books? A Thing You Only Read At School.** The trend revealed in Bunbury's study has been confirmed in other ways. Since 1982, I've been running courses for students who need help with university reading and writing. In terms of standardised testing, all except a few of these students score in the top stanine on the College Level of the Degrees of Reading Power Test (College Board, Chicago University), yet the naturalistic data which I collect during my association with them reveals that they are a special kind of **illiterate literate**, what I call the **A-literate** (the A is shorthand for 'alienated from'). Among other things, these data reveal that many of them have a distinct distaste for sustained engagement with the specialised and technical prose typical of textbooks.

In their interviews with me, they tell me things like this:

I know I have to learn from this economics textbook and I've set aside an hour a day to read it, but the same thing happens every day. After about ten minutes I feel drowsy and nothing goes in. Why do textbooks have to be so boring? Perhaps I've got — what is it? — er, dyslexia or something.

When I observe them engaged in such reading and ask them to describe by thinking out loud what it is that they are doing, one thing becomes obvious — many of them appear to be reading the text in the same way that they would read a pulp novel or a popular magazine. The concept of actively engaging with the text in order to learn from it rather than be entertained by it seems quite foreign and, to many, an unattractive idea. ('You mean I gotta read it if it's boring?') This distaste for sustained engagement with text seems to begin in the primary school. Some data on attitudes towards reading collected by Noel Logan and myself in 1983 *(Logan & Cambourne, 1983)* showed a dramatic and steady decline in children's positive attitudes towards reading between Grades 2 and 8 in a large, stratified sample of children in the second largest school region in New South Wales.

23

While these kind of data are not revealed by the surveys which show that levels of literacy have improved, if they reflect a general trend (and I'm convinced that they do), they are cause for some concern. Of what use is it to produce school graduates whose standardised test scores indicate that, when forced to, they can read, but who do not turn readily and continually to books and other forms of text as sources of learning, information or even entertainment? Of what use is it to produce school graduates who see reading as a school-based, not a lifelong activity? Of what use is teaching a skill like reading if it has such a low durability that it ceases to be used, and in some cases is actually avoided, when schooling is over?

Habit-Formation Learning and the Teaching of Writing

The picture with respect to the writing side of literacy learning is a lot more depressing. Some five years ago, I copied a procedure which I saw Frank Smith use on a class of mine which he took as a guest lecturer when visiting Australia. I remember him asking my class three questions about their own writing practices.

> 1. *Do you like writing?*
> 2. *How many pages of writing would you do each day,* ***voluntarily?***
> 3. *Are you good at writing?*

The results were interesting. It was a class of practising teachers enrolled in a Masters' programme. All of them answered, 'No' to question 1, 'None' to question 2, and 'No' to question 3. I was intrigued and decided to adapt the questions and use them on as many different audiences as possible.

One audience has been every new intake of students in the teacher education courses I've taught since that time. I have now collected responses from approximately 1200 students over a five-year period. From year to year, the results have been depressingly similar. Between 90-95% of freshmen students have responded similarly:

> 1. 'No' *(I don't like writing.)*
> 2. 'None' *(Who'd write voluntarily?)*
> 3. 'No' *(I don't think I'm any good at writing.)*

Another audience has been teachers whom I've addressed at workshops and seminars. Their response pattern is similar. Yet another audience has been parents whom I've addressed at parent meetings and school council meetings. Again the results have been similar. Although the number of teachers and parents involved has been fewer than the freshmen students (about half as many), they have been substantial. I feel secure in asserting that the majority of graduates of our school system, and in the case of teachers, our teacher training institutions, have very negative attitudes about themselves as writers and about the act of writing. I have tried to interview, in depth, as many of the total population of freshmen students as possible in order to find out more about these negative attitudes. Over a five-year period I've talked at length with approximately 200 students about their writing. I have been depressed by what they reveal. Among other things, they express a very strong sense of alienation towards the act of writing, manifested by an almost manic avoidance of writing tasks. They have the view that writing is a necessary evil, a part of education which one needs to tolerate, an unpleasant barrier to be negotiated before a degree can be awarded. My depression stems from the fact that these are the responses of that small proportion of the school population which has performed well enough at secondary school to be admitted to tertiary studies. The students who have these attitudes are the **successes** of the school system! That large section of the school population which does not gain entry to the university or college system would, I suspect, be equally, if not more, negative about writing.

A-Literacy Appears to Rain (sic) OK?

This state of affairs is apparently not restricted to Australia. In the introduction to a national literary competition for children between the ages of 6 and 16 in Britain, Hughes made the comments which follow *(Hughes, 1975)*. It is important to know that the competition had occurred annually for twenty years and that some 50,000 children entered it each year. After commenting on the abundance of talented writing which was submitted, he continued thus:

Looking over these pieces, anyone must wonder: What happens to all this talent? One of the curious facts about this competition which has now been going on for so long, is that so few have emerged in their adult life as writers . . . Perhaps it merely confirms that children's writing, for one reason or another, is a thing apart. One wonders, however, whether the reason might not be a sinister one . . . The statistics become even more curious when we remember that among the individuals who do later become outstanding writers, very few show more than a rudimentary talent up to their adolescence . . . the suspicion remains that we are talking about an unhappy, not to say disastrous, state of affairs where this immense biological oversupply of precocious ability is almost totally annihilated before it can mature. What is the future of a society, we wonder, that manages to lobotomise its talent in this way? Can anything at all be done about it? (Hughes, 1975)

Why does Hughes describe this as a 'disastrous state of affairs'? Why does he appear to be so concerned about society 'lobotomising its talent in this way'? I think it's because Hughes has the same fears that I have about the long-term result of what I've called 'textual alienation'. The 'disastrous state of affairs' alluded to by Hughes is, in my opinion, the fact that so many of our school graduates have not learned to use writing primarily as a tool of learning. Rather, they have been alienated from it and the subsequent loss of learning potential which is never realised because of this alienation could be, for society as a whole, cognitively and affectively, 'disastrous'.

While there are no data on the long-term effects of the lack of sustained engagement with the written form of language, it is not difficult to establish a tentative link between regular and sustained engagement with text, and cognitive functioning. For example, it's more than coincidental that those societies which discovered and used some form of writing during their history (e.g. all western technological societies) seem to have developed quite differently from those which did not (e.g. the Australian Aborigine and the many tribal cultures of New Guinea). The reading research literature contains many examples of strong, positive relationships between certain kinds of cognition and reading ability. The opposite is also true. There is research which shows that non-literate persons' performances on certain kinds of cognitive tasks can be quite different from that of their literate peers. The prospect of a society in which all but a minority of the population exhibits a high degree of textual alienation is a frightening one. Birnbaum and Emig hinted at the political ramifications of underdeveloped or unevenly developed literacy skills in a literate society when they commented thus:

> *Throughout history, reading and writing have been regarded as politically dangerous. Why else have slaves, prisoners and other minorities and majorities been denied the opportunity to read as well as write? But writing stays the far more worrisome and incendiary process. A reading citizen can come to comprehend and criticise societal mores as well as governmental acts and decisions. But only a citizen who elects to write can cause genuine trouble, can become the radical, the revolutionary. A reading citizen stays a client, a consumer of a culture; a writing citizen becomes its creator or destroyer.* **(Birnbaum & Emig, 1983)**

I am not suggesting that society is on the brink of collapse. Far from it. I am suggesting that there is a worrying increase in the incidence of graduates of our school systems who are alienated from sustained engagement with text. I am suggesting that such textual alienation effectively 'depowers' one in a society which values literacy.

I am suggesting that this textual alienation is a function of how literacy has been taught. I am suggesting that how literacy is taught is a function of the models of learning which teachers who teach literacy carry around inside their heads. I am suggesting that the model of learning which the majority of them do, in fact, carry around inside their heads is some variation of the learning-is-habit-formation model which is based on research that involved rats running mazes and dogs salivating to the sound of bells.

Finally, I am suggesting that there is another, more effective model of learning which can be applied to the learning of literacy, a model based on the way that human brains create meaning in the real world of language use.

4

An Alternate View of Learning

I regard this chapter as the most important one in the book. In it, I try to explain how I believe effective learning occurs. It is a pivotal chapter in the sense that just about everything else which is said in the book revolves around the ideas which are introduced in it.

Two Assumptions

The principles of learning which are described in this chapter are based on two assumptions, which, like the axioms presented earlier in the book, need to be brought out into the open and discussed.

1. The oral and written forms of the language are only superficially different.
2. Learning how to talk, i.e., learning how to control the oral language of the culture into which one has been born, is a stunning intellectual achievement, almost universally successful, extremely rapid, usually effortless, painless and durable (in the sense that once having mastered talk, those who have learned it continue to use it and develop it).

I will elaborate on both of these points and then draw some conclusions about learning to become literate.

1. The Oral and Written Forms of the Language are Only Superficially Different

By 'superficially different' I do not mean 'trivially different'. I'm using superficial in the sense of 'on the surface' not in the sense of 'unimportant'. Of course the two modes of language differ in many complex and interesting ways. Of course the two require different kinds of knowledge which learners must acquire in order to operate with and on them. Of course there are certain aspects of the use of the written mode which require specific knowledge which can't be carried over from the oral mode and vice versa.

However, in terms of how the brain processes them, at the deep levels of production and comprehension, there are no differences of great moment. Reading, writing, speaking and listening, while different in many respects, are but parallel manifestations of the same vital human function — the mind's effort to create meaning. The fact that speaking and listening are tied to the production and/or comprehension of patterned sequences of sound, while reading and writing are tied to the reception/production of graphic marks, is not of such great importance at the level of how the brain goes about creating meaning with them.

In terms of reception, i.e. listening in the oral mode and reading in the written mode, once past the eye or ear, the sound waves (oral mode) or light waves (written mode) which set the processes of meaning construction in action are reduced to the same basic sets of neural impulses. The same neural processes are involved, using the same neural machinery. With respect to the production of meaning (speaking/writing) the texts which are created for others to hear or read originate in the same parts of the cerebral cortex, traverse much the same kinds of neural pathways, using much the same kinds of neural processing, before the organs of production (tongue/hand) go into action. While the ease with which the organs of production can be brought under control may differ — speaking is easier than writing — this difference is also a superficial one.

So What? What Does this Mean for Literacy Learning?

These are important assumptions. If they are valid (and I'm not the only one who thinks they are: see *Smith 1979;* the work on sentence understanding by *Wanner 1973;* much of the work of the psycholinguists of the 60s, *Fodor, Bever & Garrett 1965*; and many others), it's not such a huge, intellectual leap to accept that the brain can also **learn** to process oral and written forms of the language in much the same way, **provided the conditions under which each is learned are also much the same.** (Please keep this notion in mind, for I intend to return to it later.)

2. Learning to Talk is a Stunning Intellectual Achievement

Learning to use and control the oral version of the language of the culture into which we're born is a successful, easy and painless task. It occurs with such monotonous regularity and success that we take it for granted, overlooking the enormity of the task which is regularly achieved by each normal infant which is, or ever has been, born.

It is important to ask just what is involved in learning to talk. What is it that has to be learned in order to learn one's language? At the general level the answer to this question is quite straightforward. When one has learned to control the oral version of one's language, one has learned literally countless thousands of conventions. Each language spoken on Earth today (some three or four thousand) comprises a unique, arbitrary set of signs, and rules for combining those signs to create meaning. These conventions have no inherent 'rightness' or 'logic' to them, just as driving on the right or left side of the road has no intrinsic rightness or logic to it. Yet each language is an amazingly complex, cultural artifact, comprising incredibly complex sets of sounds, words and rules for combining them, with equally numerous and complex systems for using them for different social, personal and cognitive purposes. All of this complexity must be learned by the individual members of each language community.

One gets an inkling of just how complex a system a language is, when one tries to map the grammatical rules that a native speaker of English must know implicitly when he can use, for example, the reflexive system of English. Imagine you have the task of programming a computer to produce and/or comprehend simple sentences involving a reflexive transformation. That is, the computer has to produce and/or comprehend only acceptable reflexives such as *I wash myself, you wash yourself, he/she washes him/herself, we wash ourselves, etc.* and reject aberrations such as *I wash himself.* I can assure you that it would involve you in a most demanding form of cognitive effort — I had to do it for an undergraduate assignment once! On the other hand, while they may not be able to state the rules, most four-year-olds have learned to use and understand reflexives without much obvious effort on their part.

The rules which describe how reflexives are used represent one tiny segment of all of the knowledge that speakers of English come to learn to control. Imagine that complexity and that quantity multiplied perhaps a millionfold and you'll get some idea of how incredibly complex and detailed is the oral form of the language. Yet little children with extremely immature brains have been learning it successfully for thousands of years. What is even more impressive is that they seem to have most of it under control by the time they are about five or six years of age. ***How could learning to control the written form of the language be considered any more difficult, complex or demanding than learning to control the oral form?***

How do they do it? Most of those who work in the field of language acquisition/development will argue that they do it because they're human. They will state quite simply that the Director of the Universe (whomsoever she might be) has designed us with a nervous system that has been specially programmed to learn language. And this is true. There is no other species on earth which is capable of learning a language to the same degree. However, I believe that there is more to it than merely being neurologically designed or genetically pre-programmed to learn language. There is, for example, evidence that humans who are born with that amazing piece of neural equipment we call a nervous system sometimes do **not** learn to talk, or have great difficulty in learning to do so. Inevitably the cause for such a failure can be traced to the environmental conditions in which the potential language learner is placed.

As recently as 1970, a child, called Genie in the scientific reports, was discovered who had been confined to a small room under conditions of physical restraint, and who had received only minimal human contact from the age of eighteen months until almost fourteen years. She knew no language and was not able to talk, although she subsequently learned some language. *(Curtiss, 1977)*

It seems that this amazing potential for language learning, which is part of all human equipment, needs certain conditions to prevail before it can be realised. If we were able to identify these conditions we could ask two important questions about learning to control the written mode:

(i) Are the conditions which prevail when the oral form of the language is being acquired, typically present when the time comes for formal literacy instruction?
(ii) Can they in fact be applied to the learning of literacy?

In what follows I intend to explore what these conditions might be and then to assess their relevance and applicability to the teaching and learning of literacy.

Learning to Talk:
Conditions which Made It Successful

Newly-born members of any society have no foreknowledge of the language culture into which they're born. If they are to become full members of that culture they are faced with the task of working out how to make meaning using the same language conventions that the rest of the community uses. As stated above, there are literally thousands of items of knowledge about the sound system, the vocabulary, the grammar and the social uses of language which must be learned. This is a daunting task but fortunately, over the millennia, a pedagogy has been developed which maximises the probability that the task will be successfully completed by the overwhelming majority of the community. This pedagogy is one which perfectly matches the contours of the contexts in which the learning takes place, i.e. it fits in with the social, physical and emotional parameters of what could be called the 'family unit'. Although the family unit differs from culture to culture and has differed from age to age, there are certain core features which seem to be constant across time and cultures.

For example, the young learners are always in close proximity to proficient users of the language. Furthermore, among these proficient users (the 'experts') there is usually at least one with whom the learner forms a significant bond. Most probably there is a range of 'experts' of different degrees of language proficiency with whom bonds can be formed. There is a community of 'user experts'. Within this framework there are certain conditions present which contribute to the learning processes which take place. Figure 1 is an attempt to capture these conditions in flow chart form.

My intention is to elaborate briefly on each of these concepts.

IMMERSION

From the moment they are born, young language learners are saturated in the medium they are expected to learn. The older members of the culture, the language 'experts', make available to the new members of the society thousands upon thousands of examples of the medium. For most of their waking time infants are within hearing distance of others using what it is that they are

A Schematic Representation of Brian Cambourne's Model of Learning as it applies to Literacy Learning

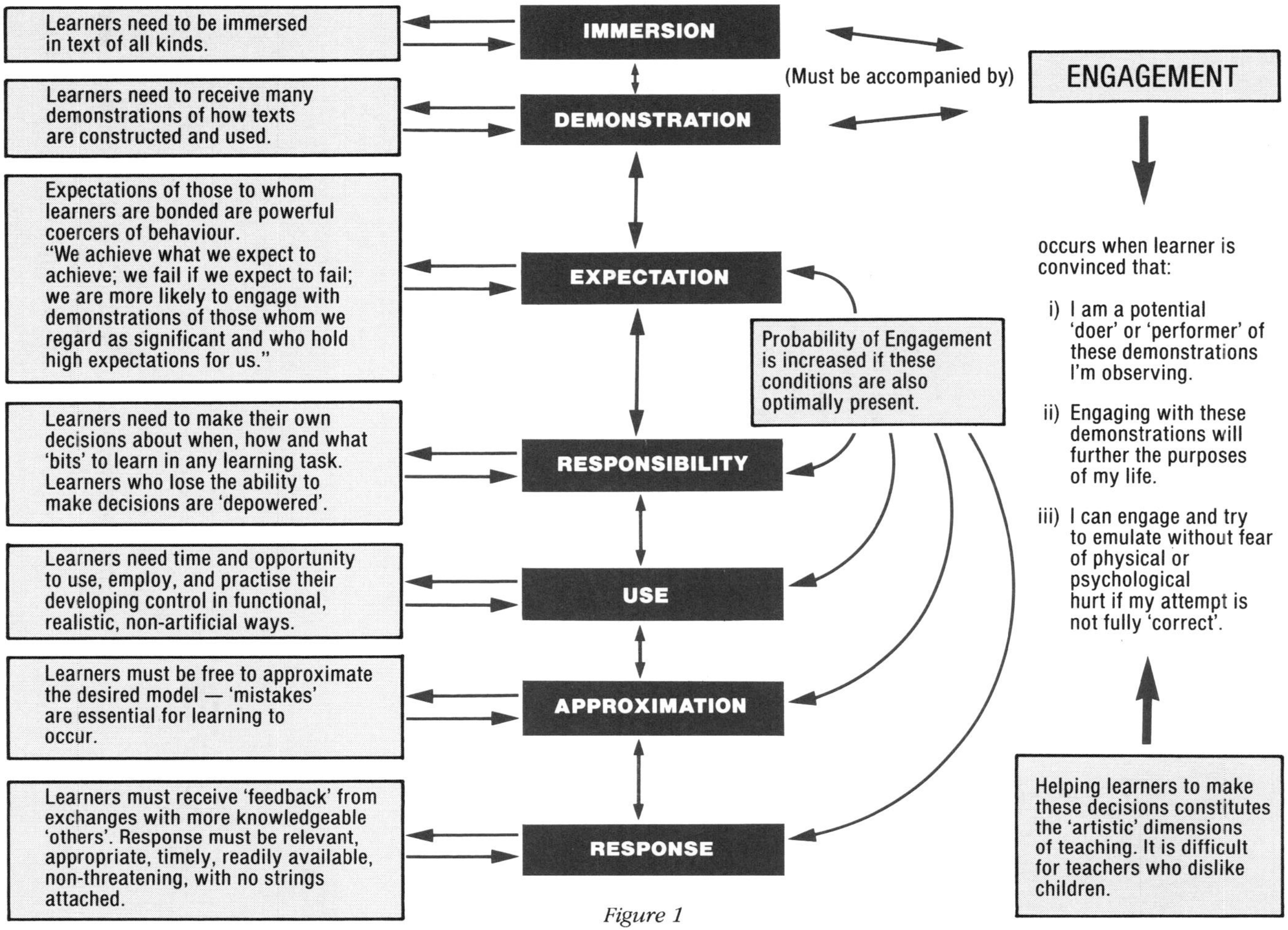

ENGAGEMENT

occurs when learner is convinced that:

i) I am a potential 'doer' or 'performer' of these demonstrations I'm observing.

ii) Engaging with these demonstrations will further the purposes of my life.

iii) I can engage and try to emulate without fear of physical or psychological hurt if my attempt is not fully 'correct'.

Helping learners to make these decisions constitutes the 'artistic' dimensions of teaching. It is difficult for teachers who dislike children.

(Must be accompanied by)

Probability of Engagement is increased if these conditions are also optimally present.

IMMERSION

Learners need to be immersed in text of all kinds.

DEMONSTRATION

Learners need to receive many demonstrations of how texts are constructed and used.

EXPECTATION

Expectations of those to whom learners are bonded are powerful coercers of behaviour.
"We achieve what we expect to achieve; we fail if we expect to fail; we are more likely to engage with demonstrations of those whom we regard as significant and who hold high expectations for us."

RESPONSIBILITY

Learners need to make their own decisions about when, how and what 'bits' to learn in any learning task. Learners who lose the ability to make decisions are 'depowered'.

USE

Learners need time and opportunity to use, employ, and practise their developing control in functional, realistic, non-artificial ways.

APPROXIMATION

Learners must be free to approximate the desired model — 'mistakes' are essential for learning to occur.

RESPONSE

Learners must receive 'feedback' from exchanges with more knowledgeable 'others'. Response must be relevant, appropriate, timely, readily available, non-threatening, with no strings attached.

Figure 1

33

expected to learn. Other members of the community either talk at them or are talking around them. Before the new arrivals are probably aware of what is going on around them, they are being exposed to the sounds, rhythms and cadences of what it is that they must ultimately learn. It is important to appreciate that what does saturate them, that which is available and in which they are immersed, is always whole, usually meaningful and in a context which makes sense or from which sense can be construed.

DEMONSTRATION

Demonstrations can take two forms. They can be actions or they can be artifacts. Father asking at the breakfast table, 'Will you pass the sugar, please?' and the subsequent passing of the sugar is not only a demonstration of what that particular sequence of sound means but also a demonstration of what language can be used for, how it functions, how it can be tied to action and so on. Young learners receive literally millions of demonstrations of what the spoken form of language means, does, sounds like, can be used for and so on. These demonstrations are the raw data that young learners must use in order to tease out how the language which they must learn is structured. I've come to believe that demonstrations are the raw material of nearly all learning, not only language learning. Potential bike riders need demonstrations of how a bike is ridden before they can begin bike riding. The same applies to shoelace tying, singing, reading, writing and spelling. Demonstrations can also be provided through artifacts. A book is an artifact. It is also a demonstration of what a book is, what print is and does, how words are spelled and how texts are structured. Demonstrations are necessary conditions for learning to occur. Without them learning will not occur. However, while necessary, demonstrations are not in themselves sufficient. Before learning can occur, a process which Smith *(1981)* labels 'engagement' must occur.

ENGAGEMENT

Learners are exposed to thousands of demonstrations each waking moment of their lives. However, a high proportion of these demonstrations merely wash over them and are ignored. Accordingly, learning will not occur. Learners will only engage with demonstrations under certain conditions. Among other things, before engagement will begin, learners need to be convinced of the following:

(i) That any demonstration which is witnessed must be perceived as 'do-able' or 'owner-able' by them. In other words, potential learners must see themselves as potential talkers, readers, bike riders, writers and so on.

(ii) That emulating the demonstrations they've witnessed will somehow further the purposes of their lives.

(iii) That attempting to emulate the demonstration will not lead to any unpleasant consequences if they fail.

What leads learners to be convinced of the wisdom of engaging with any particular demonstration or set of demonstrations? I believe that the notion of **expectation** has something to do with it.

EXPECTATION

Expectations can be talked about from a number of different perspectives. In one sense, the term can refer to the expectations that the learner holds about himself as a learner. As hinted at above, learners must believe that what they are setting out to learn is actually learnable **by them**. Smith has argued that young learners actually believe that they are capable of learning **anything** until they're convinced otherwise. *(Smith, 1981)*

In another sense, expectations can refer to what 'significant others' communicate to learners. If those to whom the learner is bonded behave in ways that communicate the message that certain kinds of learning are expected, then that learning usually takes place. Try asking the parents of a very young child whether they expect their pride and joy to learn to talk. Pay attention to the kind of response that you get!

Expectations are subtle and powerful coercers of behaviour. The research literature is replete with examples of the ways in which expectations of significant others can influence learner behaviour. Young learner talkers receive very clear indications that they are expected to learn to talk and that they are capable of doing it. Never are they given any expectations that it is too difficult a task or that it is beyond their capabilities. Expectations can also work against learning. For example, in our culture there is an expectation that swimming is dangerous, difficult and beyond young children's capabilities. Consequently, at the annual state-sponsored swimming lessons that are offered to young children each summer, about half of those who are enrolled do not learn to swim.

RESPONSIBILITY

When learning to talk, learner talkers are left to decide (take responsibility for) which particular convention or set of conventions they will attend to and subsequently internalise in their repertoires. Their 'tutors' don't try to sequence what the learner should learn. Instead they give off very strong expectations that the task will ultimately be completed. They also continue to provide high saturation and to give meaningful demonstrations. However, the learner himself or herself is left to decide just what part of the total task will be internalised at any one time.

In order to understand this notion, one must view language in a particular way — namely, as a network of interlocking systems, all of which operate simultaneously. Atwell *(1983)* describes this network with an effective visual metaphor.

Atwell's Visual Metaphor

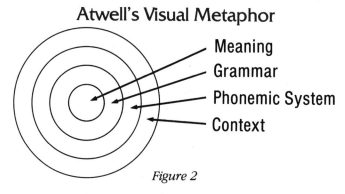

Figure 2

Oral language has an inner core of meaning which is wrapped in outer layers of grammatical, phonemic, pragmatic systems. It's a little like a transverse section of a coaxial cable. Any natural language act cuts across all these systems. For example, the demonstration referred to earlier, ('Pass the sugar, please') could be represented using the same metaphor.

Extension of Atwell's Visual Metaphor

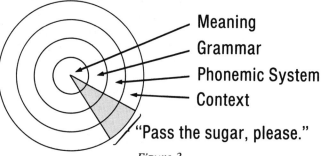

Figure 3

All the linguistic and sociolinguistic systems are present. Ultimately, the learner must come to know them all. The significant others in his environment give off very strong expectations that full learning will occur eventually. Usually, the vast majority of learners respond and full learning does occur. When a learner engages with a demonstration such as this hypothetical one, the tutor has no way of knowing which layers will be attended to, engaged with and ultimately learned. Will the learner 'hook into' the phonemic rules from this demonstration or perhaps the grammatical conventions? Then again, there are the sociolinguistic rules of breakfast behaviour. All the tutor is certain of is that, ultimately, all of it will be learned. What is important is that which is demonstrated and that which is available to be immersed in, is always a whole slice of the 'language pie' with all of the systems present.

While the tutor has the responsibility for supplying the demonstrations and for providing the climate of expectation, the learner has two levels of responsibility. Firstly, he is expected to become proficient in the total act; this is not negotiable — he **must** eventually learn to talk. Secondly, he is expected to make decisions about the most useful aspect with which to engage from the demonstration which he is currently experiencing. It's my belief that once we take this responsibility away from the child by predetermining which layer he should or can learn, and then isolate it from the others, we begin to complicate the process of learning by decontextualising and fragmenting the language act. We also begin to trivialise language.

APPROXIMATION

When learning to talk, learner talkers are **not** expected to wait until they have all the systems and sub-systems fully intact before they're allowed to talk. If this were the case they would not begin to produce audible speech until they were nine or ten years of age at the earliest. Carol Chomsky found some linguistic structures which are typically not under control until about this age *(Chomsky, 1968)*. Young learner talkers are expected to have a go, i.e. to attempt to emulate what is being demonstrated, and their childish attempts are enthusiastically, warmly and often joyously received. There is no expectation that fully developed, 'correct' (fully conventional) adult forms will be produced. In short, 'baby talk' is expected, is warmly received and treated as a legitimate, relevant, meaningful and useful contribution to the context. Nor is anxiety displayed about the unconventional forms which proliferate in baby talk. If any direct intervention is given, it is given only when the teacher adult (parent) thinks the 'truth value' of what the learner talker is trying to say is compromised. The learner points to a truck and says, 'Dat car.' When the truth

37

value is **not** compromised, direct instruction on a particular error is not given, e.g. 'You omitted the verb to be (is) and the indefinite article (a). Say after me, Dat is a car.'

Furthermore, there is no anxiety that the immature attempts of the adult form will become permanent fixtures of the learner's repertoire. On the contrary. Those who are responsible for the learner's language development know and expect that the immature forms will drop out and be replaced by conventional ones. And they do. What is more, they have been doing so for as long as children have been allowed to produce language.

This willingness to accept approximations is absolutely essential to the processes which accompany language learning. In fact it sets in motion the 'hypothesise, test, modify hypothesis, test again' cycle which characterises all natural learning. Modification of hypothesis can only occur, if as a consequence of testing the hypothesis, some 'unrest' sets in train the reformulation of the hypothesis and so on. Without the condition of ready acceptance of the approximations, the whole hypothesis/test/modification cycle would not occur. Neither would learning. The processes shown in figure 4 would simply not occur if error-free perfection was demanded prior to employment.

USE

Young learner talkers need both time and opportunity to use their immature, developing language skills. They appear to need both time and opportunity to use their language with others, as well as time alone, away from others to practise and use what they've been learning. Ruth Weir's classic study of the pre-sleep monologues in which young children run through portions of their ever-increasing linguistic repertoires is an example of this form of use *(Weir, 1962)*.

RESPONSE

I used to refer to this as **feedback**. I've switched to **response** because the term feedback has mechanistic and behaviourist overtones. It also implies a predetermined purpose on the part of the feedback giver. My data *(Cambourne, 1972)* convince me that parents are not consciously aware of the 'giving feedback' function which their exchanges with children serve. Rather, these exchanges appear to serve the function of the 'sharing of information' about both the language and the degree of control that the learner has over it at any one time. When the learner talker says, as he points to a cup on the table, 'Dat cup,' the response from the parent, if indeed it is a cup, typically goes something like this, 'Yes, that's a cup.'

How Learning to Mean "Proceeds"

(The "Processes" Involved)

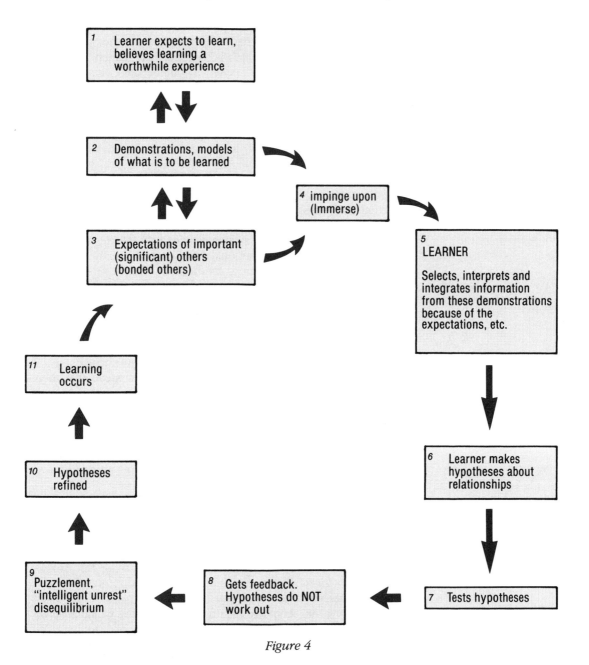

Figure 4

What is being exchanged here? The parent is supplying the missing bits of the child's approximation. The child is supplying the parent with an example of what he is currently capable of doing. It is interesting to look back through a 'bugging' study of mine and note what the parents did **not** do in these mutual exchanges. For example, the child who says to the parent 'Dat cup,' or something similar, was never given any specific information about the errors which had been made. No parent in my data ever made specific reference to the nature of the auxiliaries, indefinite articles or the pronunciation of 'th'. The information which is shared by the 'expert' in this kind of situation is a **full** (as opposed to fragmented) version of what the learner attempted. It is as if the expert intuitively understands the importance of responsibility and says to himself, 'I've no right to decide which aspect of this learner's approximation should be attended to right now. Therefore I'll give him the conventional version of what I think he wanted to say and leave him to decide which aspect he'll attend to and adjust.'

While exchanges may vary in detail and richness from parent to parent and sub-culture to sub-culture, they have certain things in common: a) they are readily available, frequently given, non-threatening and **with no strings attached**; b) there is no penalty for not getting the conventional form correct the next time it is produced. There is no limit to the number of exchanges which are offered and given.

Quite often the expert in these exchanges provides a scaffold for further language learning to occur, 'Yes, that's Daddy's blue cup, isn't it?', thus keeping the conversational game going and providing more opportunities to employ, practise, hypothesise, specify, elaborate, generalise and so on. This does not mean that there's not an implicit contract involved (remember expectations), or that it's merely potluck learning. It's a very specific form of contextually specific learning which aims at maximum impact.

The thesis presented in this chapter is not new. In fact, as long ago as 1898 a Miss Harriet Iredell argued thus in an article she wrote for the magazine **Education**.

When we have command of a language both in its spoken and written form we pass impartially from one to the other. Whether we hear a thing or see it; whether we speak or write, there is to the mind no sense of difference in the fact. Since the two forms of the one mode of expression are so alike in themselves and in their psychological and practical use and effect, it would seem that the principles and rules which govern the acquirement of the one, must govern the acquirement of the other, and in the natural order of things they would be learned alike. So much depends upon the truth or falsity of this, that the question claims earnest and immediate consideration. *(Iredell, Education, 1898, pp 233-238)*

I can understand how learning to talk is natural, but learning to read and write . . . how can that be natural?

While learning to talk (that is, learning to control the spoken form of language) is seen as a 'natural' form of behaviour by most people, there is not the same agreement that learning to read and write (that is, learning to control the written form) is as 'natural'. There are even some who would argue that learning to read and write **cannot** be described as a natural form of behaviour at all.

The reasons for this are obvious. Talking is a universal medium of communication. Every culture has an oral form of language which every member of that culture strives to learn, sometimes against overwhelming disabilities and handicaps, e.g. blind, deaf, or mentally deficient children. The stream of everyday, ongoing behaviour keeps providing opportunities for all new members of a culture, i.e. recently born children, to use their developing language for purposes other than learning it. As a consequence they seem to learn to control it as a by-product of using it.

The same cannot be said for the written form of the language. The real world does not naturally provide the same kinds of opportunities for the written form of the language. Of course, in our print-saturated society it is possible to argue that demonstrations of how the written form of the language can be read might, under ideal circumstances, be naturally provided by the environment. For example, adults reading stories to young learners who can see the print, mothers reading the supermarket print while their infants watch and so on. But there are very few contexts in the real world where writing is the major medium of communication, where young learners can engage with it in much the same way that they can engage with demonstrations of the spoken form. The very strong need in our society to be error-free — to meet all the conventions of written language before producing a text for public consumption — means that before one really engages in acts of writing, one must know how to do it first, otherwise it cannot possible be error-free. This is a paradox which I haven't quite explained satisfactorily for myself. Furthermore, writing is perceived mainly as a medium of communication. It is usually performed in special settings, (offices, classrooms, libraries) in isolation. All of these factors must militate against the skills of writing being learned as a by-product of using it. The real world simply does not provide the conditions for learning to write that it provides for learning to talk.

41

But surely this is not a valid reason for not attempting to simulate, for the written form of language, those conditions which made learning the oral form possible?

The only reason for **not** trying to simulate for the written form what we know happened when young learners set out to learn the oral form, would be to assume somehow, that the written form of the language **cannot** be learned under the same conditions even if they are provided. I find this argument difficult to sustain, for it assumes that learning is either a topic-based or process-based phenomenon. It assumes, in other words, that while one can learn to talk under the conditions of learning described above, a completely different set of conditions is needed for learning writing or maths or singing or art or playing the piano or science . . .

I find it much more satisfying to believe that there is a single, unitary, very effective process of learning which is exemplified by learning to talk and, that over the long period of human evolution, the brain has evolved so that it prefers to learn this way and that most learning, especially language-related learning, proceeds most effectively under these conditions.

What we need to realise is that while the 'natural' world provides the opportunities for oral language learning processes to go into action, it does not provide them for other kinds of learning, especially learning to read and write. Herein lies the function of schools. Schools are settings in which we need to create those opportunities for learning to read and write that the real, everyday world does not provide, at least to the degree that it provides them for learning to talk. Thus, when I use the phrase 'learning to read and write naturally', I'm really talking about simulating the natural conditions that we know work for learning to talk, so that they're available for the learning of reading and writing. On the surface it might seem to be a kind of paradox. I'm arguing that teachers need to simulate nature (the real world) because nature will not provide the opportunities for these other types of learning to proceed naturally.

However, there is no paradox. Just because the world does not provide the same kinds of natural conditions for learning to control the written forms of language, this is not a valid reason for trying to teach literacy by imposing conditions which interfere with the processes for which evolution has obviously prepared the brain.

In the following chapters I attempt to describe how these conditions can be applied to the teaching and learning of the skills of literacy.

5

Theory into Practice I

Transfer-ability

I'm often asked whether the conditions of learning which seem to make learning to talk so spectacularly successful can be simply and easily transferred to learning how to read, write and spell. Typically, I answer both 'Yes and no'.

I answer 'No' because **written language is not merely oral language which has been written down**. The written form of language is different from the oral form in many subtle and complex ways. For example, it is used for quite different purposes, in quite different contexts, under quite different conditions. Some researchers have even found that it coerces a quite different form of cognitive and social functioning from that which the oral form coerces. *(Scollan, 1987)*

In very simplistic terms, written discourse is structured differently from oral discourse. The rhythms, cadences, organisational and structural characteristics of written texts are not only quite different from oral texts, they can be quite different from each other. Narrative is different from report which is different from argument, and so on. Those who have learned to control the spoken form of language and who wish to learn to use and control the written forms must learn to make use of a whole new set of linguistic options which underlie these rhythmic, organisational and structural characteristics of different written forms. Please note that when I use the phrase 'learn to control and use the written forms' I include both modes of literate behaviour, reading **and** writing. Just as it would be impossible for anyone to use all the spoken registers which are used in any community (1 still can't understand the register used at cattle auctions), so it is impossible for anyone to learn to control all the registers of written language which exist. Those which teachers decide to teach their pupils will be a function of what the teacher believes to be important. That is, those language forms she values and knows about.

I answer 'No' because I know that it is impossible in the real world to provide a **precisely identical** set of conditions for the learning of literacy. The degrees of immersion; the frequency, quality and range of demonstrations; the opportunity for demonstrations; the obvious value and 'worthwhileness' of learning to control the written form of the language; the relationships with, and range of, significant others; the time to use and practise; the frequency and nature of the responses given — in fact, all of those conditions described in the previous chapter, can never be **exactly replicated** for the written mode of language.

The reasons are obvious. The oral form of language is 'natural' in the sense that the real world seems to have been designed to make the acquisition of the oral forms of language maximally probable. Human societies are ordered and structured in such a way that the conditions which I described in the previous chapter are continually and constantly present. The immersion, demonstration, expectation, etc. seem to occur as by-products of everyday human activity; the world is constantly providing demonstrations of the purposes, functions and structure of language for those who must learn it. The response, the readily available 'talker experts', the feedback, etc. are by-products of the ebb and flow of everyday social intercourse. It is as if the core elements of human society have been especially designed to guarantee that oral language will be learned.

The world does not provide the same privileges for the learning of the written mode. The world does not throw up the same kinds of demonstrations of, or provide the same opportunities for, immersion in the written mode of language. This means that the best we can do if our culture subscribes to the development of literacy, is to **simulate** for the written mode those conditions of learning that existed when the oral mode of language was being learned. But we can never hope to reproduce the exact, identical set of conditions that made learning to talk possible.

I also answer 'No' because I know that there are subtle differences of degree in the learning of the two modes. Because I have watched so many learners both learn and fail to learn to gain control of the written form of language, I realise that learning to control the written mode of language seems to be facilitated if the learners develop high degrees of what I've called 'meta-textual awareness', that is, the ability to reflect upon and talk about the ways that the written form of the language 'works'. There is an oral language equivalent of this ability but it is not so obvious. For example, when children are engaged in learning to control the oral form of language they do reflect upon the metaphors, similes, riddles, jokes, etc. that occur in their linguistic contexts. This is a kind of meta-linguistic behaviour, which seems to help young learner talkers come to grips with some of the finer nuances of oral language use. With respect to the written form of language, it seems that it has to be more intense. There appears to be a requirement for the learner reader/ writer to make certain conscious links between the oral and written forms of language.

I answer 'Yes' because I believe that while the conditions for learning to talk cannot be precisely replicated for the written mode of language, the principles which they exemplify can.

I answer 'Yes' because when teachers understand the principles they can and do arrange their classrooms so that they simulate for the written form of the language what the world appears to do naturally for the oral form. When they do this, the learning which occurs is both powerful and durable.

Translating the Conditions of Oral Language Learning to Literacy Learning

The learning theory which lies at the core of this book argues that immersion in different written forms is one of the necessary prerequisites for learning to use and control these forms. This argument applies equally to very young learners learning how to read and write simple recounts and narratives as it does to more sophisticated learners trying to master the registers of academic argument in different disciplines, or to businessmen reading and/or writing company reports.

IMMERSION

Immersion, when applied to literacy learning, can take a number of forms. At the most general level it can be either visual or aural — I think it should be both. At another level it can be teacher-controlled immersion or learner-controlled immersion.

Filling the walls of the classroom with labels, song charts, poem charts, nursery rhymes, weather charts, labelled art and labelled craft artifacts which learners move amongst and use every day, is one form of visual immersion. Such immersion is usually teacher-controlled in the sense that she usually decides what forms the charts will take, how many there will be and where they will be located.

It is important that child-made charts be at least as numerous as those made by teachers.

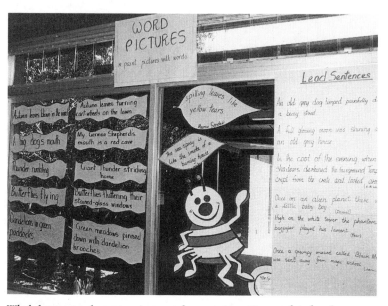

Whole language classrooms immerse learners in written and spoken language.

Teachers reading to children and thus saturating them with the rhythms, cadences and sounds of written language is an example of **teacher-controlled aural immersion.** Providing the time and the resources for the learners to immerse themselves both visually and aurally through the reading of self-selected texts would be an example of **learner-controlled visual and aural immersion.**

The concept of immersion carries with it the notions of 'opportunity for' and 'availability of' text to be engaged with. It also brings with it the notion of variability of text form. Furthermore, immersion which is long and deep will be more likely to be effective than that which is shallow and quick; a quick dip at the ocean's edge is qualitatively different from the long swim.

Immersion, it seems, needs time. It needs a variety of text forms to be available for possible engagement by learners, and it needs to be both visual and aural, as well as being both teacher- **and** learner-controlled.

Immersion is more than a simple teaching 'activity' or 'strategy'. It is an underlying pervasive or 'overarching superordinate' condition which becomes part of one's teaching consciousness and which permeates most of the planning decisions, the resource allocation decisions and the budget decisions which teachers frequently need to make.

DEMONSTRATION

Demonstrations are artifacts and/or actions from which we can learn. Seeing someone tie a shoelace is a demonstration of how shoelace-tying is done. Seeing someone ride a bike is a demonstration of how bike-riding is done. Hearing a stream of sound from someone's mouth at the breakfast table and seeing the sugar passed across is a demonstration of what that stream of sound means and what it can be used for. Seeing someone read a book or compose a note are demonstrations of how one reads or composes. A book is an artifact which contains demonstrations of how words are spelled, how sentences are punctuated, how different text forms are structured and so on. The world is filled with demonstrations and if we engage with one of them we internalise some aspect or portion of that particular demonstration. If we engage with repeated demonstrations of the same action and/or artifact we begin to select other aspects of it to internalise and, as a consequence, we begin to interpret, organise and reorganise our developing knowledge until we can perform and/or produce that demonstration or a variation of it. This is another way of saying we learn.

If demonstrations are necessary conditions for learning to occur, then classrooms should be places where learners are exposed to a multiplicity of relevant and functional demonstrations. The problem for teachers of literacy is knowing enough about the total processes of literacy to be able to develop and present a range and variety of demonstrations that will enable learners to select, interpret, organise and re-orient, etc. their developing literacy knowledge into patterns and schemas that will eventually make them fully literate.

This means that appropriate demonstrations are possible only from informed demonstrators. While I can offer no finite list of 'literacy demonstrations' suitable for pre-school or Grade 1, etc. there are some general principles I can offer for consideration.

Demonstrations need to be demonstrations of language 'wholes'.

All this means is that the literacy act or artifact being demonstrated needs to be whole enough to provide enough information about the various systems and sub-systems of language so that the learner, if he decides to engage, will have the data available for working out how all the pieces fit together and interact with each other. For example, a teacher standing in front of her class with an overhead projector and a blank acetate who says, 'I'm going to show you how I compose and draft an official note to parents about the next school council meeting,' and then proceeds to think 'out loud' as she composes and drafts, is demonstrating a whole range of skills and knowledge about an act of literacy. Depending on what she actually says as she 'loud-thinks', she could demonstrate any combination of, or all of, the following:

— that writing proceeds from left to right and top to bottom,
— what letters look like,
— how full stops and capital letters are used,
— how paragraphs are formed,
— how official notes are structured,
— how words can be phonemically segmented,
— how ideas are sequenced,
— how grammar works to aid meaning and purpose.

In whole language classrooms, teachers are continually demonstrating how reading, writing and thinking are done.

Any learner engaging with this demonstration has available, if he wants or needs it, a great deal of information about how the various systems (phonemic, syntactic, semantic, pragmatic, graphic) of written language 'fit' with each other. If the teacher's loud-thinking also makes explicit the 'why' of what she does by reporting what she is thinking as she does it, the learner is also getting a demonstration of the meta-textual knowledge that she is using to guide and control her writing behaviour.

On the other hand, a teacher who gives a demonstration of how to make the sound that the letters /a/r/ make in a list of unrelated words, is not demonstrating how the process and knowledge of blending 'ar' fits in with the act of reading or writing or spelling or generally being literate. Demonstrations which emphasise only one or two of the sub-systems of language and de-emphasise or even ignore others which typically accompany them, make learning less comprehensible and therefore more complex.

Demonstrations need to be continually repeated.

Demonstrations of whole slices of language or language behaviour typically contain so much information that potential learners cannot hope to take in all of the bits that make it up after just one demonstration. Demonstrations need to be repeated again and again to allow for engagement and re-engagement to occur until the learner has taken sufficient from the demonstration to make it part of his repertoire of skills and/or knowledge. This does not mean that the same demonstrations need to be repeated monotonously over and over again, ad nauseam. One of the interesting things about language is that the same information can be made available through a multiplicity of different forms of language. A shared book lesson demonstrates many of the same aspects of language and/or language use as does sharing one's writing or talking about a book which has been read or watching someone else read or listening to someone talk about a book which they've read. This means that repeated demonstrations can be continually given in a multiplicity of ways using a multiplicity of materials. Demonstrations which are exactly the same do not have to be repeated. The same information, skills and processes can be made available through quite differently constructed demonstrations.

There is no ideal length for a demonstration.

Theoretically, everything which occurs in a classroom is a demonstration. Learners will engage with them if they happen to be relevant to their particular needs or interests. Reading a book in serial form for 20 minutes every morning is a demonstration of how reading is done, how text is structured and what books do. If, during the reading, the teacher also demonstrates how she deals with difficulties in the text by taking ten seconds to think out loud, thus:

"Oops! Here's a word I don't know *(spells)* /s/c/a/l/d/i/n/g. I'll just say 'something' and go on and see if I can work out what it means."

She is also demonstrating a range of literacy behaviour and knowledge with which learners can potentially engage. If, while reading, she takes a further ten seconds to point out how Colin Thiele has used a whole string of similes to achieve a certain effect, she is demonstrating something about authorcraft.

Demonstrations: a final word

Classrooms need to provide a smorgasbord of **contextually-relevant demonstrations.** A contextually-relevant demonstration is one which is appropriate to the particular literacy task that a learner is trying to complete. A classroom which continually provides contextually-relevant demonstrations is not unlike a cafe which serves a smorgasbord menu. Like a diner at a smorgasbord-style dinner, a learner can move amongst what is being made available, sampling here and there, (metaphorically) nibbling at something which looks (cognitively) appetising, filling his (metaphorical) plate from those dishes (demonstrations) that best satisfy his needs at that particular time, ignoring those which have no appeal at the time but all the time knowing that there are plenty of dishes to which he can return again and again until his hunger is satisfied.

ENGAGEMENT

While immersion and demonstration are **necessary** conditions for learning to occur, they are not in themselves **sufficient.** This means that potential learners can be deeply immersed in some medium like music, art or written language, and receive innumerable high quality demonstrations of how music, art, writing, etc. are 'done', yet not seem to learn much at all about music, art, reading, writing and so on. Despite the immersion and demonstrations learning does not seem to take place.

I want to suggest that the reason for this state of affairs is that something is missing from the learning equation. The missing factor is what Frank Smith calls 'engagement' *(Smith, 1981)*. It's a compelling concept. The picture which I get in my mind when I hear it used in the context of talking about learning is of the clutch on an old-fashioned motor car **engaging** the motor as it is slowly released, thus connecting the power of the motor to the drive shaft of the car and setting it in motion. This clutch analogy can be spun out a little further. Car engines can be revved very unproductively, i.e. no movement of the vehicle will take place, while the clutch is in a 'not engaged', i.e. neutral, position. Engagement, or the connecting of the power of the motor to the mechanisms which produce movement, is absolutely essential if movement is to occur. Immersion and demonstration without engagement can be compared to the useless revving of a motor. The 'clutch' of learning needs to be connected to the 'power' of immersion and demonstration if there is going to be any learning 'movement'. Without the learner's engagement with the demonstrations which are made available by the persons or artifacts which surround/immerse him, they will wash over him and pass him by. Learning from such demonstrations thus becomes highly unlikely.

We've all encountered the child who never seems to learn what it is we're trying to teach him, despite the immersion and the demonstrations which we give him. Usually, we attribute his failure to some inherent weakness or perversity within him, and in one sense that could be right. In some learners there appears to be either an inability or a refusal to engage with what we try to demonstrate. The mistake we make (I think) is that we attribute this inability or refusal to factors which are either physiological or psychological in origin. And on the surface it **does** appear that learners either **refuse to** or are **unable to** engage with our demonstrations or with the media in which they're immersed because of some factor or combination of factors within them. We would do better, I believe, to regard it as having more of a socio-historical origin. At a deeper level, I believe that it's got more to do with the way they have been treated as learners rather than any inherent or deep-seated weakness in their make-up.

In order to understand this, one needs to understand how and why engagement takes place. Why is it that some learners seem to engage with our demonstrations and others don't? The fact that the overwhelming majority of persons who are born learn to talk the language of the culture into which they've been born, means that they must have engaged with many of the demonstrations of language being used and many of the samples of language in which they were immersed. Why? Why do they decide to engage with the noise of language and to try to use it in the ways in which it has been demonstrated to them and not with the noise which, for example, the air conditioner makes? If we could answer these questions, then we may get some insights into what factors cause engagement to occur.

The Why and How of Engagement

Here's an interesting question: ***What are the factors which determine whether or not learners will engage with the demonstrations that teachers offer them?***

Surely this is the question that cognitive 'engineers' would dearly like to answer. Just imagine — if there was a sure-fire way of ensuring that learners would engage with just those demonstrations that we had carefully worked out as being optimal for some learning outcome to occur, we could pre-package learning modules, i.e. sets of demonstrations, merely present them and *presto!* Perfect learning, perfectly controlled by the learning engineer. This is the chimera which behavioural psychologists and the Direct Instructionists have been chasing for years. They've failed because they've not understood the concept of **engagement**. Typically, they've confused it with the notion of 'motivation'.

Here's what I think they've failed to acknowledge or understand:
  i) Learners will not engage with a demonstration unless they believe that they are potential 'doers' or 'owners' of that demonstration. Before learners will engage with the demonstrations which occur around them each waking moment of their lives, they must see themselves as potential doers of whatever is being demonstrated. They must see themselves as potential bike riders, shoelace tiers, users of the language, readers, writers and so on. If a learner cannot envisage himself thus, or if he believes that he is not capable of ever learning or mastering whatever is being demonstrated, engagement is unlikely to occur.
  ii) Learners will not see themselves thus unless simultaneously they also believe that by becoming 'doers' or 'owners' of the behaviours or skills or knowledge being demonstrated, they will somehow further the purposes of their lives. This is more than simple motivation although it has some overtones of the pure sense of motivation. This is why kids will persevere with learning how to talk. The contexts in which they live and move are filled with examples of how acts of talking and communicating do further the purposes of life.
  iii) Learners will not engage unless the risks associated with engagement are sufferable and liveable through, that is, from an emotional perspective. All engagement involves a risk but if the risks are perceived by the learner to be unendurable or threatening in any way, then engagement will be avoided.

Here's an example of these three principles from my own experience:

I love to watch the hang-gliders soaring above the cliffs near the university. The grace and freedom they're obviously experiencing and the sheer adventure of what they're doing forces me to observe them every time they're around. They fascinate me, and the spectacle they present is extremely compelling for me. I am rivetted to the displays they put on. I observe their demonstrations with an awestruck incredulity. But I don't engage with these demonstrations.

There is a difference between compelling observation and a motivation to watch an interesting spectacle and the decision to learn anything from (i.e. engage with) that demonstration. I simply do not see myself as a potential hang-glider. I know that the demonstration I am fascinated by and will travel miles to observe is something that I am not a potential 'doer' of. I know that my age and my state of physical health and fitness would make it highly unlikely that I will ever attempt it. Furthermore, I truly cannot see how taking up hang-gliding at this stage of my life would ever further the purposes of my life. At this stage of life, what I believe will be 'good for me' is firmly established and has been worked out over the years through all of the experiences, both pleasant and unpleasant, that I've had.

Finally, the prospect of taking the risk and actually getting into hang-gliding fills me with terror. I'm quite certain that I would crash and, if not kill myself, probably become a quadraplegic!

Although I'm a fascinated observer of demonstrations of hang-gliding, I do not engage with them. If someone asked me to draw an accurate representation of a hang-glider, or to describe the materials from which one is made, or to describe the appendages and straps and harnesses that are an integral part of it, or even to describe the markings on it, I would be hard put to do so. I have observed. I am fascinated, 'interested' and highly motivated to watch but I have not engaged and learning of any significance has not occurred.

This partly explains why some learners appear to be unteachable in some subjects. Stated very simplistically, they have not been able to make the kinds of decisions which lead to engagement. Perhaps one of the artistic dimensions of teaching in any subject area, but especially in literacy, is somehow setting up conditions and relationships which will increase the probability that learners can make the kinds of decisions that lead to engagement.

There is one other factor associated with engagement that I'd like to raise — the probability of engagement is increased if the demonstrations are given by a person with whom the learner has bonded. This is especially so with respect to learning to talk. The demonstrators are, in the main, those persons with whom the learner has formed a very strong bond — mothers, fathers, grandmothers, siblings, etc are always 'significant others' in the young learners' lives. We are continually modelling ourselves on those whom we admire, respect and like. In short, we tend to engage with demonstrations given by those whom we want to emulate. All this can be captured by the following set of principles.

Principles of Engagement:

Deep engagement with demonstrations is maximised when learners are convinced that:

i) they are potential doers of whatever is being demonstrated. (**Implication** — we must avoid giving potential learners the message that they are incapable of ultimately learning what is being demonstrated.)

ii) engaging with what is being demonstrated will further the purposes of the potential learners' lives. (**Implication** — we must convince potential learners that attaining high degrees of literacy is really one of the most important things in their lives, more important even than drugs, sex or booze.)

iii) engagement with whatever is being demonstrated will not lead to pain, humiliation, denigration. (**Implication** — potential learners must feel safe to have a go.)

Learners need to believe that they are potential doers of whatever is being demonstrated if they are to learn.

There is a corollary to these three principles:

iv) Learners are more likely to engage with the demonstrations provided by those who are significant to them. (**Implication** — on the one hand, significant persons, such as parents, need to give the appropriate demonstrations that support literacy development and acquisition. On the other hand, those charged with providing the relevant demonstrations, such as teachers, need to become significant persons to potential learners.

What Does this Long Treatise on Engagement Mean for Teachers?

There are several messages for teachers.

Teachers need to convince learners that they like them.

If teachers treat learners in ways that signal that they dislike them and think poorly of them, or in ways that result in the learners perceiving teachers as people who could never be 'significant others' in their lives, then the probability of learners engaging with the demonstrations which teachers provide is minimal. There are a multiplicity of ways in which teachers can ensure that they will **not** become significant others in learners' lives:

★ By being grumpy, remote, uncaring, unloving, spiteful, sarcastic, denigrating, threatening, punitive and negative about the learner's world and the learner's attempts at any learning task.

★ By communicating to learners that any demonstration which they (the teachers) provide will be inextricably bound up with them and their negative views of the world.

When put in a class with a teacher who manifests any of the above behaviours, learners with even a modicum of common sense will arrive at the following conclusion:

> That's not for me. I don't want to be like that, or emulate that, or even be reminded of that way of approaching the world or learning or literacy or whatever it is that the demonstration is associated with. That's a person whom I don't wish to emulate. That's a person whose demonstrations I refuse to engage with.

Teachers need to be conscious of the nature of the demonstrations which they give.

If teachers want to maximise the probability that engagement will occur, then they need to be aware of the nature of the demonstrations which they are giving their charges, particularly those demonstrations associated with the specific content and processes that they have decided they want children to learn.

Teachers need to be conscious of the nature of the demonstrations which they give.

What does the material which is used in classrooms demonstrate about the nature of reading and writing? That it's a meaningful, relevant enterprise with a solid, meaningful and functional base? Or that reading is essentially nonsense or hard work or something that is always either right or wrong or boring or something that you only do at school? Or that writing is difficult or complex or usually has something wrong with it when you do it or is used as a punishment or is a set of fragmented skills that somehow you must first get under control and somehow or other orchestrate after completing trivial, 'dummy' exercises.

Teachers need to be aware of those factors which determine engagement.

At another level, the teacher needs to be aware of the factors which affect engagement in learners, in particular with regard to the setting up of those conditions which optimise the probability that engagement will occur. How do you convince learners that they are potential readers, writers or spellers? (Remember the first decision that learners must make about any demonstration which they witness?) Simple. You **expect** them to do so and you communicate this expectation in all of your dealings with them and with the notions and processes of reading and writing and spelling, etc. When these expectations are met, or even partly met, you rejoice and celebrate the enormity of what has been learned with the learner, just as you did when you helped your own child learn to talk.

However, merely exhorting teachers to 'expect' and claiming that these expectations will be fulfilled may sound a bit glib. How does one 'expect'? How does one communicate these expectations? In order to answer these questions we need to look a little more closely at the notion of 'expectations'.

EXPECTATIONS

How do expectations manifest themselves in the natural learning classroom?

Expectations are messages that are communicated to learners in a variety of very subtle ways. They are somehow connected with the confidence that a teacher consistently displays in her learners' abilities to be ultimately successful in whatever they are trying to master.

Displaying confidence in another person usually has very positive connotations. It usually has overtones of liking, affection, even love. Confidence is difficult to express when there are overtones of dislike or even when there's a kind of neutral lack of enthusiasm expressed towards another.

What does this mean for teachers?

The implicit message communicated by a teacher who has high expectations of learners under her care is this:

> I am extremely confident that you have the ability and the skill to eventually master the skills and/or processes that you and I and the rest of your peers in this class are setting out to master. Furthermore, I think you are a worthy and likeable human being with many fine, unique and valuable qualities which make you a special person. I like you and value you and I will joyously receive and respond to the gains you make, no matter how small.

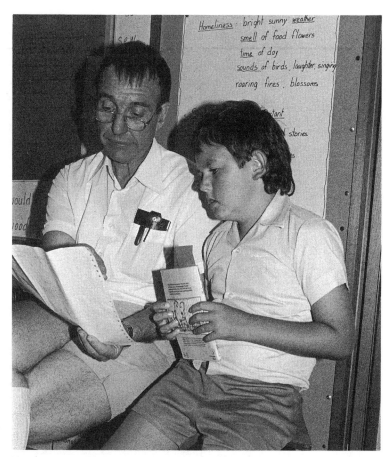

Teachers must communicate positive expectations to learners.

There is another kind of expectation that needs to be communicated. As well as expectations about learners' abilities, there is also a need to convey this message:

> Whatever it is that we're trying to learn is worthwhile, valuable, relevant, extremely functional and useful.

This means being able to convince learners that reading is a worthwhile activity, that writing is not only easily learned but is extremely empowering and useful and so on. It means **never** behaving in ways which might lead learners to expect that reading and writing are subjects which are done each day because there's a slot for them on the timetable. A teacher's dislike for, or apathy towards, any domain of learning, no matter how carefully one attempts to conceal it, is immediately communicated to learners. The message which they receive goes something like this:

> I don't really expect you to enjoy this. I don't, so why should you?

What about negative expectations? How are they avoided?

Perhaps the best way to deal with this question is to explain it from a negative perspective. How might one set out to convince potential learners that they will have great difficulty in learning the skills or concepts associated with becoming literate? Here's a set of strategies which are guaranteed to produce negative expectations in learners:

How to Give Off Negative Expectations

★ By grouping learners in ways that make it patently obvious to them that they are not successful learners, e.g. the Wombat Group syndrome.

★ By not trusting learners to make decisions.

★ By reducing learners' experiences to a small subset of the total experience and explaining that they have to learn the little bits first before they can attempt the whole act.

★ By telling learners that whatever they're setting out to learn is hard, difficult or too complex.

★ By providing the evidence that this is so by setting meaningless, trivial tasks.

★ By continually pointing out learners' failures and then making them rework their errors, ad nauseam.

★ By demonstrating that the tasks of reading, writing and spelling are so difficult and complex and meaningless that there is little point in even trying to learn them.

★ By saying things and behaving in ways which communicate to a learner these messages:

— You're dumb. I really don't think you can do this.

— Look at all the things you haven't yet got under control.

— Look at your mark (assessment, etc.) compared with so and so's.

— This is too hard for the likes of you.

— You're in the special group that needs extra (baby) work.

— While the rest do this, I want you to go to Mr X's room for special (baby) help.

— Here are all the errors I've found in your attempt, now correct them.

— Three sentences is all Grade 1 can write.

— I don't really value you as a person or a learner.

— You're a pest and you spoil my day by your very presence here.

— I don't think you'll ever amount to anything much.

Expectations: a final word

Expectations are very closely related to building high self esteem in learners and developing a loving and trusting relationship with them. The knack is to be able to convince learners that we are genuine and not false about the expectations and positive feelings and attitudes we have towards them and whatever it is we happen to be teaching. It's also a little mixed up with enthusiasm for our subject and the degree to which we can make this enthusiasm contagious.

What I've been talking about above are what I call 'global expectations'. There is another level of expectation that teachers need to be conscious of — namely, the individual expectations that they hold for each individual child in their care. Thus, what one pupil produces for the teacher may be far superior in all respects to that which another produces, yet the one who produces the superior work may be given this kind of message:

"Todd, that's not your best effort. I know you can do better!"

Meanwhile, the one who produces work which is quite inferior to that which Todd produced receives a highly enthusiastic response which is filled with praise and positive messages:

"Jesse, that's really very good. Look at how much you've learned in the last week!"

Expectations at the individual level depend on how well the teacher knows each of her pupils. Without a very clear awareness of what each individual child is capable of doing, this second level of expectation cannot be applied.

**Get to know your pupils, so that your expectations
at the individual level are valid.**

There is a danger that these notions could be interpreted to mean that teachers necessarily have to be milksop approvers of anything and everything any learner produces. This is not so. Teachers' responses must be genuine and if they do not like or approve of a learner's attempt then they are bound to let the learner know. In short, expectations can also have a hard edge to them. Two plus two does **not** equal five; it is, from a meaning perspective, quite wrong. Similarly, there are conventions of spelling, punctuation and so on which, while possessing little of the inherent 'rightness' or 'logic' of mathematics, nevertheless have to be met. These are 'hard-edged' expectations. The necessity of meeting them ought to be clearly and unambiguously communicated to learners.

RESPONSIBILITY

The notion that learners should 'take responsibility for their own learning' is a difficult one to explain to many teachers. For many of them it smacks of abandonment of professional responsibility. For many it carries connotations of directionless learning, of children in classrooms doing only what's enjoyable for them, of not 'knuckling down to the hard facts of the world'. It raises the issue of how young learners could possibly know what's best for them. As one teacher said to me, 'If we let kids take responsibility for their own learning, how can we be assured they will learn what's best for them?' It also raises the spectre of thirty or so learners all doing their own thing. This, of course, poses an impossible situation in a classroom which has a lock-step curriculum. It also presents an impossible situation for teachers who hold a view similar to that which I described earlier as 'the original sin theory of learning', i.e. if left to their own devices, children will only learn what's bad for them.

Comments such as those raised above reflect an interpretation of 'responsibility' which is quite different from mine. To me, the concept of 'taking responsibility' in the learning process involves two basic kinds of behaviour:

a) Learners displaying a willingness to make decisions about learning, independently of the teacher.

b) Teachers trusting learners to engage with demonstrations which are made available and to select from those demonstrations what they, the learners, decide is necessary for them to learn or experiment with at that particular time.

Teachers must trust learners to engage with, and select from, the demonstrations which are made available.

These two kinds of behaviour are, after all, what happens in the learning that takes place outside the formal classroom. In the kind of learning which is continually occurring in the world, what each individual actually learns is not organised by some omniscient, celestial teacher into a carefully worked out sequence of stages or 'bits'. With respect to the kinds of demonstrations which they receive, learners of all levels of maturity are treated by the world in the same way. The world simply doesn't provide specially tailored demonstrations for learners of different stages of development and knowledge. It simply provides demonstrations. It's up to the learners who experience the demonstrations to decide what it is that they take from each demonstration, if they take anything at all.

Thus, the same demonstration will be treated quite differently by different learners and each will take something different from it. For example, imagine two brothers, one aged four and one aged two, sitting at the breakfast table with their mother and father. Dad makes a request: 'Pass the sugar, please.' Mum complies by passing the sugar.

Let us hypothesise that both young learners attend to and engage with some aspect of this demonstration. It is obvious that each would not engage with exactly the same part or parts of the demonstration. The two-year-old may focus on some aspect of the phonological or morphological features of the demonstration, testing out what he heard with what he has been trying to produce in his own speech. The four-year-old, however, may decide that the tone of voice or the form which the request takes is more pertinent to his current language learning needs.

Young language learners have been accustomed to taking this kind of responsibility, to making these kinds of decisions since they were born. They have also been accustomed to having 'teachers' (parents, siblings and other family) who both expect and allow them to take this kind of responsibility especially with respect to language learning. It would be reasonable to argue that this kind of behaviour appears to be a natural part of learning. While both the learners and the 'teachers' may not be consciously aware of this responsibility, the ways in which both learners and teachers behave towards each other in the learning to talk process make it abundantly clear that the kind of responsibility I'm describing is part of the learning contract that exists.

With respect to learning to talk, children have been expected to be responsible for their learning, and have made many independent decisions about what 'bits' of the oral language puzzle they attempt to solve at any particular time. School learning is probably their first experience of someone else deciding for them what shall be learned and when it shall be learned. In this sense it is probably their first experience of learning which does not conform to what they have been doing prior to attendance at school. It is probably their first taste of what I call 'aberrant learning' — learning which is not what the brain has been designed to do.

What does this view of responsibility mean for teaching?

It means that traditional approaches to programming — preplanning a common set of learning tasks and/or activities — becomes a logical impossibility.

It is naive to think, for example, that all learners will need a demonstration on the same day at the same time of how fullstops are used! Such decisions by the teacher inevitably lead to the learner **not** making his own independent decisions. It is probably the beginning of what I call 'dependent learning' for some children, i.e. they become dependent on someone else directing their learning. I am reminded of the students I encounter at university who demand to be given what they call 'structure'. What they are really asking of me is a set of steps showing what they should learn for their exams. Sadly they've lost the ability to make decisions about their own learning. They don't feel comfortable unless someone else is directing their efforts.

It means that textbooks with so-called 'graded' exercises or kits with carefully worked out sequences of sub-skills are based on dubious premises.

Teachers, textbook writers or kit developers cannot really predetermine a sequence of steps or 'bits' of reading or writing learning that learners need to learn in a certain 'optimal' order. The view of responsibility presented above makes the old educational aphorism of moving from the simple to the complex in an engineered way, invalid. 'Simple' and 'complex' are relative terms based on the logic of someone who has already mastered reading or writing. They are not terms based on the 'psycho-logic' of the learner trying to piece the whole puzzle together. As Frank Smith once said, the teaching of phonics always makes great sense to someone who already knows how to read.

I've observed lots of young non-readers trying to understand phonic instruction which is removed from the context of reading and writing. The evidence I've collected over the years convinces me that they do not find it 'easy' or 'logical'. What teachers or textbook writers or kit designers or worksheet producers design as the next 'logical' step in the movement from simple to complex, is not necessarily the next 'psychological' step for every learner in the room. While it is true that learners do, in fact, proceed in their learning from what is simple **for them** to what is more complex **for them**, it is not true that teachers or experts who publish programmes and textbooks can fragment the language act into the next most appropriate complex 'bit' for each and every one of them. Attempts to predetermine the sequences of activities and/or demonstrations that learners, en masse, should receive, has resulted in de-naturalising the learning act for all but those who, by some fortuitous coincidence, are ready for what the demonstration provides. This must result in complicating learning unnecessarily for the majority of learners.

It means that demonstrations must be demonstrations of 'wholes' of language behaviour.

If teachers want learners to make decisions about which part of a demonstration they will engage with, teachers must provide demonstrations which contain all the information from which any learner may wish to draw. If as many of the interacting systems of language as possible are present in any demonstration, then the learner who engages is forced to make choices concerning just what aspects of language he will focus on and internalise.

It means being prepared to provide similar demonstrations over and over again.

If, during one demonstration a learner engages with and learns one part of the written language puzzle, he needs similar demonstrations to learn how other bits of the puzzle fit together. In other words, as one set of conventions or ways of using language are mastered, the learner needs other opportunities to focus on different parts of the puzzle. Independent learners, i.e. those who can be responsible for their own learning, need the assurance that once they get one bit of language under control, the opportunities to get the rest will be readily and frequently available.

What this view of responsibility does NOT mean for teachers.

Fully mature, adult, self-motivated, self-directing, autonomous learners can choose to learn or not learn, can seek out what it is they need to learn and can choose to ignore what they don't wish to learn. Some teachers assume that 'responsibility' means permitting young, underdeveloped learners to behave in a similar fashion. This is not what I mean. Giving responsibility to the young learner in school does not mean that he can choose not to learn. Nor does it mean that the teacher simply stands back and expects the immature learner to take responsibility for searching and finding what it is that he must learn. Nor does it mean that he can choose to engage with just those things in which he is interested. At the infant and primary level of instruction it means having to make decisions about learning — but not all the decisions.

It means being given practice in making decisions that are commensurate with one's state of knowledge and skill. Thus, ten-year-olds in a classroom may be working a contract system which sets certain, basic, teacher-chosen parameters around the content and amount that they learn but within which there are six to ten options from which they can choose. This leaves certain important decisions and choices to be made about the way the learners spend their time, and the actual material they work on. Less mature learners may need far fewer options. I've worked with some children who can only make a decision between two options. This I regard as far better than having none. At least some decisions are being practised and some responsibility being taken when choosing between two options. Too often young learners are not given any.

What sorts of things can teachers do to promote responsibility in learning?

There is no exhaustive list of things to do which can be readily supplied. However, here are a few things to keep in mind:

★ As far as possible, refrain from telling learners how to spell words, recognise words or write sentences until they've 'had a go' first. Always insist that they have a go before they can ask for help.

★ Make explicit the knowledge that learners learn best if they have a go first and then seek help.

★ Make it a rule that learners use peers to help them solve problems before they use teachers. The experience of trying to teach and/ or explain something to someone else is probably one of the most effective ways to make decisions about learning. It's probably also one of the most effective ways to learn. Teachers should be the last resort in solving a learning problem.

★ Make it a rule that peers only help with the process of solving the problem, not with the solution to the problem itself. Rather than telling a friend how to spell 'house', show him where the word may be found in the room.

★ Organise classrooms so that options which depend on choices being made are an integral part of the learning environment. For example, in any learning session learners should be expected to choose whether they will work on A, B or C, all of which must ultimately be worked on and completed in due course.

APPROXIMATION

Approximation is one of the conditions of natural learning which teachers find easiest to understand but most difficult to implement. While they can understand how the notion of approximation applies to the acquisition of the oral form of the language, they find it extremely difficult to apply it to the written form of the language. Why?

Firstly, because there is a very strong consensus in our culture about correctness and error avoidance. Most teachers and parents — in fact, almost everyone who might be included in the 'general public' — have a very strong conviction that an integral part of learning is the rooting out of an error before it becomes too firmly established. As I mentioned earlier in the book, this is a spin-off from the 'learning is habit formation' view of learning.

Secondly, most people never relate the learning of oral language with the learning of the written form of the language. Unless the processes of approximation which baby-talk encapsulates are brought to their conscious attention, they never pause to reflect on what happens naturally to every person who has ever learned to talk.

The evidence is quite unequivocal. Learning to control the appropriate oral forms of language proceeds through a series of successive approximations with the learner receiving information about the success or otherwise of his attempt and modifying his behaviour accordingly. When learning is looked at as a form of hypothesis testing, it becomes obvious that approximations (errors) are absolutely essential to the whole process. Figure 4, repeated below, shows the process in flow-chart form.

How Learning to Mean "Proceeds"

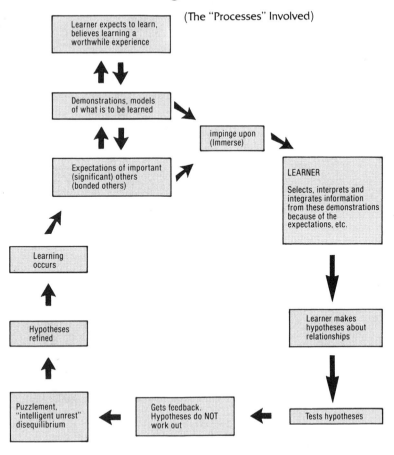

(The "Processes" Involved)

This figure depicts how a learner engages with a demonstration of some action or artifact because a significant other in his life expects it of him. These expectations are conveyed to the potential learner. The learner has also been convinced, both as a result of the demonstrations he's witnessed and from the way he's been treated, that he is a potential doer/owner of that demonstration, that it will further the purposes of his life, and that he is safe to have a go. He knows that if his attempt is not quite right, he will not be treated badly or humiliated, nor will his ego be bruised or damaged in any way.

When a learner 'has a go', sooner or later his attempt is open to public scrutiny by another.

It is obvious that having a go (being free to approximate) is crucial to the process of learning. When a learner has a go, his 'go' sooner or later becomes public. All that this means is that his attempt is open to public scrutiny by another. In the learning to talk situation, this 'other' is usually someone who has more control over whatever it is at which the learner is having a go. When this happens, the learner must face the inevitable fact that his hypothesis may not be quite correct. When this happens it becomes necessary for him to re-engage with the demonstration, or one similar to it, and adjust his hypothesis. This cycle is repeated over and over until the demonstration is his, is part of him and he can know and/or do whatever the demonstration entails.

Without the opportunity to approximate, the whole, smooth-running learning cycle is stopped and progress and/or refinement becomes impossible.

What are the effects of not permitting approximations?

What are the effects of insisting on perfection from learners when they first set out to learn something as complex as gaining control over the written form of language? There are two answers to this question.

1 It produces safe behaviour, that is, keeping within the framework of what one already knows and rarely venturing outside that framework. It results in learners who never expose themselves — learners who rarely progress because they rarely try themselves out.

Having a go, taking a risk or daring to be wrong in an environment which ensures that your approximation will be warmly and joyously received, is fundamental for learning to occur. Without the freedom to approximate, no progress in learning can be achieved. This applies to learning at all levels. The infant learning to spell, the graduate learning to write a doctoral thesis — all learners need the opportunities to gradually work their individual ways towards whatever finished product or process they're trying to master.

2 It results in what can be labelled 'get-it-right-first-time' teaching.

If the right to approximate in one's learning is removed, the logical consequence is that one must get whatever is being learned correct the first time one attempts it. This is what I call 'get-it-right-first-time' (GIRFT) teaching. What are the consequences of get-it-right-first-time teaching? Firstly, it means that the natural cycle of learning is severely interfered with. When GIRFT applies, there is a strong expectation that the potential learner will engage with the demonstration in such a way that all of it, in toto, will be internalised. This notion that the total demonstration, every part of it, must be learned, lends itself very much to a fragmented view of learning. It's not difficult to work out why. Even the most insensitive of the habit-formation learning theorists will admit the impossibility of the expectation that young learners much, for example, learn **everything** about an act of writing which is demonstrated.

Just imagine it! A teacher calls the kindergarten class together and gives a demonstration of how she writes a note home to the parents. Think of all the interlocking parts and pieces of language that she must have learned to control in order to do this; knowledge about spelling, handwriting, sentence structure, punctuation, etc. Everyone knows that no one could expect a kindergarten child to learn **all** of that perfectly in one demonstration. So what's the logical answer? Right! Break the total act down into little bits and get the child to learn perfectly (to engage with and internalise) all of the one or two small bits of the total act which have been carefully selected for him to learn, and keep him at it until it is learned 'errorlessly'.

The same GIRFT logic can be applied to learners further up the academic ladder. Let's imagine the aim of a lesson (or course or subject) is for the learner to be able to write an economics essay. If you demonstrate the writing of an economics essay with all that's involved — content, all the conventions of writing, all the aspects of the genre that's known as 'the economics essay' — it becomes obvious that no learner could typically learn all of that at once. So what's the logical answer? Right! Fragment the total act. This enables the learner to focus on the whole demonstration. He can therefore be expected to get it all right before he moves on to the next little bit, and the next little bit, and then the next little bit . . . Is it any wonder that so many of those who have been raised in GIRFT classrooms do not like writing or reading?

Freedom to approximate is an essential ingredient of all successful learning.

USE

An important part of the learning cycle is the opportunity for the learner to play around with or put into effect the hypotheses he's currently working on. I used to call this 'practice'. Then I tried 'employment'. Although I've decided that 'use' is a better descriptive term, the essence of what I mean is contained in all of these terms. In the natural learning situation, the real world 'throws up' or offers a multitude of opportunities for learners to try themselves out in contextually relevant and meaningful ways. When children are learning to talk they are constantly finding themselves in situations where what they have been learning about language needs to be brought into play and tried out. Usually this results in some kind of response being given, a response that can either extend and/or modify the learner's control of what it is that he is trying to learn.

Parents, siblings, and other proficient language users with whom the learner talker interacts are adept at setting up such situations. The range of peek-a-boo games which are played with very young learners (e.g. grandmother hiding behind the newspaper and saying "Peek-a-boo" to the child as she pops her head out, with the child repeating the same laugh-cum-intonation pattern each time) is one example in which the 'use' condition is manifested in the real world. One outcome of such games is that the same thing is practised over and over for the purpose of having fun and enjoying oneself, not for the specific conscious purpose of learning language. With older children more sophisticated 'use' strategies are evident. Two I'm aware of from my own data:

THE NAMING GAME — Mother is dressing the child. She holds up a bootie and asks, "What's this?" When the child makes a response, she supplies feedback then holds up the next item and the game continues.

THE 'TELL ME' GAME — Toddler enters the room crying.
Mother: "What's the matter? Tell me what's the matter."
Toddler: "Ball. Bobby ball."
Mother: "Bobby took your ball, did he?"
Toddler: "Yes."
Mother: "What did Bobby do? Tell me what Bobby did."

There are many variations of this game, e.g., tell Daddy, Grandma, Joanne, etc., what you saw at the park today. Tell me what you did at school today.

Play is probably the most obvious real world situation which coerces learners into using language. Role-playing games, e.g. playing school, playing mothers and fathers, playing shopping, etc., create situations which involve the participants in using (practising) a range of language forms over which they have varying degrees of mastery. The interactions which take place in such situations create opportunities for learner talkers to receive feedback about the appropriateness of what they say and how they say it. In such situations, other learners provide demonstrations through which the learner talker can engage and through which they can subsequently refine and modify how they use language.

Play can also be solitary, particularly verbal play. I have recorded speech-for-self monologues with pre-schoolers which last for over half an hour. During such monologues the children appear to be trying to recreate previous linguisitic experiences, such as words of songs, poems, chants, rhymes, friends' names, difficult to pronounce words, and so on. Weir's work on the pre-sleep monologues of young children is another example of the condition I've called 'use'. *(Weir, 1961)* The regularity with which such monologues occur, especially with toddlers learning to talk, suggests that there is a need for learner talkers to get away from the hovering supervision of their family tutors occasionally to try things out for themselves.

With respect to learning to control the oral forms of the language, the kinds of real world situations described above seem to serve at least four purposes:

1. Encouragement for young learner talkers to keep testing their hypotheses about how the language they're trying to control actually works.

2. Provision for the care-givers, and those who have the responsibility for teaching the child to talk, to receive ongoing information about the learner talker's developing degree of control.

3. Opportunities for specific language demonstrations which are related to each learner's current linguistic needs.

4. Opportunities for practice, refinement and subsequent modification of language hypotheses.

These trying-out-my-developing-language-skill situations have several important characteristics. Firstly, the use or practice which characterises them is incidental to, or is a by-product of, the major purpose of the setting or context in which it occurs. The learner has not engaged in the business of the language setting (the peek-a-boo game, the 'tell me' strategy, the cooperative or solitary play, the speech-for-self monologues, etc.) for the specific or conscious purpose of learning more about the language. Usually, there is a broader, more macroscopic reason or set of reasons which motivates the decision to participate. The fact that this broader agenda happens to involve learners using their developing language skills and actually 'going public' with them, is a fortuitous, unplanned by-product.

What is important for learning to talk is that the environment keeps throwing up settings (contexts) which allow the learner, nay, **coerce** the learner to use his burgeoning linguistic ability and get feedback about its appropriateness. Secondly, in the natural learning situation, the time is there to engage in this broader agenda.

Let me say it another way:

> In the natural situation, one learns the conventions, rules, functions, purposes and other aspects of the oral form of language as a kind of incidental by-product of the many situations in which one gets to use one's burgeoning language power. There is little or no direct instruction. There are no specific contexts set up which one could label 'learning to talk' lessons. All the learning which goes on is a by-product of some other, broader set of purposes.

The reason that this form of learning is usually so successful for oral language is patently obvious: oral communication is such an all-purpose, all-pervasive human activity that the probability of being coerced to use one's developing language power is extremely high. Consequently, the probability of receiving demonstrations of the linguistic concepts and skills which the finished or graduated learner talker has developed, and getting feedback about one's own degree of mastery of them, is also high.

How does this concept of use translate to classroom practice?

Within the settings which we call language classrooms, is it possible for teachers to provide the same or similar sets of conditions of use, with the same kinds of success — especially with respect to the written form of language?

Classrooms are settings in which there is not an unlimited amount of time. While it could be argued that the opportunities for what I've called 'learning as a by-product of use' are not as readily available in classrooms, this does not mean that they cannot be made available. How does one make them available? There is no single, unitary recipe which I can supply. Learning as a by-product of use is a consequence of the expectations communicated by the teacher, by the demonstrations provided, by the way time is divided up and used, by the nature of the activities which the teacher selects for the class and by a host of other important factors. (I shall deal with these things in a later chapter.)

Learners should experience an urgent need to read and write in order to achieve ends other than learning about reading and writing.

In short, it is a consequence of the total classroom climate which the teacher creates. The underlying principle is really quite simple:

In order to implement the principles of 'use' most effectively in classrooms, teachers need to create settings in which learners experience an urgent need to read and write in order to achieve ends other than learning about reading and writing.

The kinds of activities that learners are asked to engage in are crucial. They must be seen by the learners to be activities which have purposes that go beyond simply learning about language, or filling in time, or practising a skill.

For example, I was once asked by a concerned teacher to observe his class in action. He'd been trying to implement whole language/ natural learning principles in his classroom for about six months with limited success. He explained it to me thus:

"I've been to observe other teachers who have organised their classrooms around these principles and know it works for them. I've copied their methods of organisation and their time plans. I demonstrate, I immerse, I have high expectations, and so on. I do what they do, but I'm still fighting the kids. Sometimes they respond, other times they don't. Perhaps it only works for nice, middle-class kids?"

When I went to observe him I had to agree. He was a sincerely motivated, skilful and caring teacher. He read and demonstrated to the children, he allowed SSR each day and, in general, seemed to be modelling his teaching practice on what successful teachers in a neighbouring school were doing. It wasn't until he reached that part of his language session in which the children chose language activities to complete that I became aware of what was different.

The activities which his children were asked to do were merely time fillers. One group did a cloze activity on a passage which he had selected beforehand. Another group completed a seatwork activity on prefixes and suffixes which he'd photocopied from a text book. A third group answered some comprehension questions on a previously unseen passage. These are activities which begin nowhere and go nowhere. The children knew they were time fillers aimed at drill and practice. They saw no other purpose for them.

By contrast, the activities which children in the more successful classes did were quite different. Some of them grew out of the SSR period which typically preceded activity time; for example, designing a cover or blurb for a book they'd just finished reading **so that the librarian could display it in the library in order to inform children from other classes of what the book was like.** Or, perhaps, after having read a series of fables and fairy tales, children would be engaged in writing their own **for a class anthology to be placed in the library for other classes to read.** Then again, others could be designing a wall chart which described the criteria which identify a fairy tale and distinguish it from a fable, **in order to assist those who were engaged in the writing task.**

These are activities which involved reading, writing, talking, listening, arguing, comparing, selecting, organising, thinking — **for the purpose of completing some more macroscopic, meaningful task.**

RESPONSE

Teachers do a lot of responding. The response I'm referring to here is the response which teachers make to learners' hypotheses about the way that the written form of the language works. It occurs in that part of the learning cycle (see figure 1 on page 33) when a learner's underdeveloped or immature understandings of how the written language puzzle works are open to public scrutiny. It refers to that moment when someone who knows more about the written form of the language than the learner does, engages with the learner's approximation and lets him know either that it's acceptable or that it's not conventional and that some modifications are necessary.

In the learning to talk situation these 'response moments' have certain necessary characteristics:

1. **They are usually a by-product of a language exchange.** The learner and the expert communicate for the purposes of achieving some end and as a by-product of this original purpose there is a response which supplies the learner with information about the language forms he is trying to master.

2. **The response given by the expert is typically meaning-centred.** The expert usually responds to the *meaning* of what is being communicated, not to the form.

3. **The response given by the expert is typically non-threatening.**

4. **There is no direct attention drawn to any specific part of the learner's attempt.** Typically, the response is one which provides a demonstration in its entirety of what it was that the learner was trying to say.

The classic exemplar of this form of response is the mother-child dialogue which occurs during the 'baby talk' phase of toddlerhood. For example:

> Toddler: *(pointing to father's sock on the bedroom floor)*
> "Dat Daddy sock."
> Mother: "Yes, that's Daddy's sock."

It should be remembered that this kind of response is embedded in a climate of high expectations of the learner's ability to, ultimately, 'get it all together'. Furthermore, there is a pervading ethos that communicates to the learner that learning to control this form of communication is really a very worthwhile thing to try to do. Finally, there is unlimited time and opportunity for this kind of response to be given.

While the principles which underlie these real world responses can be applied in the classroom to the written form of the language, **they can't be replicated exactly.** This is because the contexts are slightly different. For example, when a learner brings a piece of writing to the teacher for a conference of some kind, both teacher and child know that the specific purpose for the conference is to give and receive feedback about the piece. The teacher hasn't time to engage the learner in some kind of dialogue from which some feedback about the learner's effort might incidentally emerge. Typically, the teacher decides what needs to be demonstrated and discussed about each child's written piece, and focuses directly on that. Furthermore, on some occasions the focus will be on form and not on meaning. Then again, there is a limit to the number of times that responses can be made available to each individual child in the class. Despite these differences in context, it is possible to capture the flavour of the real world responses when dealing with learners' attempts to make meaning through reading and/or writing. When reduced to their core elements, the responses which are typically made to learner talkers in the real world can be characterised thus:

Acceptance
Celebration
Evaluation (this phase is covert and subconscious)
Demonstration

In other words when learner talkers have a go and attempt to make meaning, their attempts are typically **accepted** regardless of the degree to which it matches, or doesn't match, the 'correct', conventional form. Often the acceptance is overlaid with a mood of **celebration** — mothers, fathers, grandparents, etc., display obvious enthusiasm and delight in the attempts that the young learners make to master their language. To most people, 'baby talk' is irresistibly cute and they respond accordingly. This sense of celebration and approval is also obvious to the learners who make the attempts. This is why they keep coming back for more.

Each learner talker's attempt to make language is unconsciously **evaluated** by the person (tutor) with whom they're interacting. If we take the example of "Dat Daddy sock" given above, it could be inferred that something like this has taken place inside the mother's head:

Now the baby has said, "Dat Daddy sock". That's a true statement; it is his father's sock that he's pointing at. He's probably trying to say, something like "That's Daddy's sock" but he hasn't got it quite right yet. He's still struggling with some of the conventions of grammar and pronunciation. I'm not sure just what he needs help with now, so I'll supply him with what it is that he's trying to say.

In this evaluation phase there is some evidence that parents and others also often decide that the learner is capable of a closer approximation to the conventional form, and in their response they communicate to the learner that a closer approximation is expected. ("Say that again?" "What did you say?" etc.) This has been referred to as "raising the ante" by some researchers. *(Geekie and Keeble, 1987)* A variation of this is what these researchers labelled 'applying the ratchet'. This occurs when parents and others refuse to let the learner talker regress to an earlier, less conventional form of expression. For example, a learner may try to regress to calling a dog a 'bow-wow' long after the parent knows that the adult form of the word is an established part of the learner's repertoire.

After the evaluation comes the **demonstration.** Typically, in the learning to talk situation it consists of a verbal response which contains information that the learner talker can use if the decision to engage is made.

I want to argue that it is possible, with minor modifications, to apply the principles of acceptance, celebration, evaluation and demonstration to the responses given to learner writers and learner readers in the whole language classroom.

Teachers should have no difficulty in applying the **acceptance/ celebration** principles to learners' attempts to control reading and writing. If teachers know their pupils well enough they should know whether an attempt at reading and writing is a genuine one which represents the learner's authentic state of knowledge and/or development. If it's a genuine attempt which may contain many errors but which represents what the teacher believes is a breakthrough by that learner, then it deserves to be not only accepted but celebrated as well. Celebration is manifested by displays of genuine enthusiasm by the teacher for the learner's achievement.

In the classroom context, the **evaluation** phase of the response needs to be much more of a conscious activity than it is in the real world situation. Teachers need to have a set of criteria which relate to each learner's written language development within their heads. When they respond to a learner's reading/writing attempt they must, in the space of a few microseconds, be able to apply these criteria to the learner's attempt, decide what degree of celebration is warranted, and then decide how to demonstrate what it is that the learner needs to know and/or do.

It is at the **demonstration** phase that modifications to what happens in the learning-to-talk context are most obvious. Whereas the parent or tutor in the learning-to-talk situation can give a verbal response which contains the information which the learner needs, this is not always possible in the classroom context when it is the written language which is being used. In a writing or reading conference, the teacher cannot always give, in verbal form, a demonstration of what the learner needs to know.

If, for example, the learner is struggling to write a report and the attempt which is shared with the teacher has many, many irregularities of form, spelling, punctuation and grammar, etc., the teacher cannot respond to all of these simultaneously by providing a demonstration of what the finished product should look like using oral language and conversational techniques. Nor has she time to do a quick rewrite of what the learner is attempting so that a perfect model can be handed across immediately. (Unless, of course, it's a one- or two-line effort that very young writers typically produce.) She must therefore decide what and how much can be demonstrated so that the learner can attend to some of the problems inherent in what is being attempted. In my observations of how successful, whole language teachers manage this, I've noted the following strategies being used:

(i) Focusing on gaps in learner knowledge/skill

The teacher responds to the learner's attempt to write and/or read by deciding that one or two gaps in learner knowledge or learner skill can be treated with a quick demonstration from her there and then. For example, "You've made a good attempt to write this report (read this text, etc.) but you've got some extra things to learn to do before you become perfect at it. You can't hope to learn them all at once so I'm going to show you how to organise your information (put in speech marks, put in full stops, spell words, work out unknown words, what to do when you get a reading blockage, etc.) now. Listen (watch) carefully . . ."

(ii) Extending (Raising the ante)

"This is a really good attempt to write a report (read this text, etc.). You've almost got it right. Here's something else you might like to think about. Reports are different from narratives. See if you can work out how they're different."

(iii) Redirecting to a source which will help

"You're having trouble with using the dictionary, aren't you? Melissa is really good at using dictionaries. Go and ask her to show you what she knows about using one."

or

"If you want to know how to structure a report (spell a word, punctuate a sentence, etc.), look in this book (on this wall chart, etc.)."

There are many other opportunities within the classroom in which the conditions of response applying to the oral form of the language can also be applied to the written form. Many of the responses that occur as a consequence of the peer interaction which accompanies collaborative learning activities have all of the qualities of these responses.

Just as in the family structure nature creates settings in which the feedback for learning to talk is made available, so too can the classroom be organised. In the chapters which follow, I'll try to supply some insights.

6

Theory into Practice II

Whenever I address teachers about the theory of learning described in this book, I can be certain that I will be asked some variation of this question: *How can all of this be put into practice?*

I am usually quick to answer that there is no single method of implementing the theoretical principles which I've been talking about. All classrooms are different, just as all children and teachers are different, and each context will coerce different methodological interpretations of the theory. In other words, I have no standard recipe for the implementation of this theory. There are, however, certain fundamental, practical principles which have emerged over the years, upon which other teachers might build their own individual methodologies. In what follows I shall describe some of these principles.

The Nitty-Gritty — Getting Started

The many hours which I've spent observing teachers who set out to implement what might be called a whole language/natural learning approach to literacy have convinced me that there are at least two things that need to be done before the face-to-face classroom encounters actually begin.

Firstly, teachers need to sit down at a desk and work out what I call a 'global language plan' which encapsulates and synthesises all of the theoretical principles of language and literacy learning which are described earlier in this book. Secondly, they need to establish some objectives for the learners in their class. Once these two things are in place, there are a number of other requirements which need to be worked out, including:

- the way time is organised;
- the way classroom space is organised;
- the range of resources which are needed;
- the nature of demonstrations which might be used;
- the activities which learners will engage in;
- the teacher's ways of talking and interacting with learners;
- ways of monitoring and evaluating literacy development.

Inevitably, all of these things are linked in a complex web of subtle, ubiquitous networks. A change of emphasis or direction in any one or combination of these factors leads to changes in other parts of the web.

This is what makes describing how a whole language/natural learning classroom works, so difficult. Each and every one of the categories of practical concerns listed above is not mutually exclusive. They overlap and interact in ways that make precise description of exactly **how** these classrooms can be organised and **run**, impossible. The linkages, relationships and the overlap are so pervasive that when one tries to explain or expand upon one concept or set of relationships, one finds that it becomes necessary to tie them to other concepts which haven't yet been mentioned. In other words, these classrooms are hard to describe as a linear list of events or steps. In what follows I intend to describe how teachers might go about addressing themselves to some of these requirements. My aim is to try to categorise roughly the information which I want to present under two broad headings, each of which has several sub-headings.

1. Making Decisions about How the Programme **Should** be Run

    A. Devising a global language plan
    B. Deciding literacy objectives

2. Making Decisions about How the Programme **Will** be Run

    A. Organising time
    B. Organising space
    C. Organising resources
    D. Demonstrations
    E. Developing activities
    F. Talking and interacting with learners
    G. Monitoring and evaluating literacy development

1. Making Decisions about How the Programme Should be Run

A. Devising a global language plan

The function of a language plan is to keep to the fore of one's thinking the conditions of learning which I've described earlier. Here is an example of one language plan that I know 'works'.

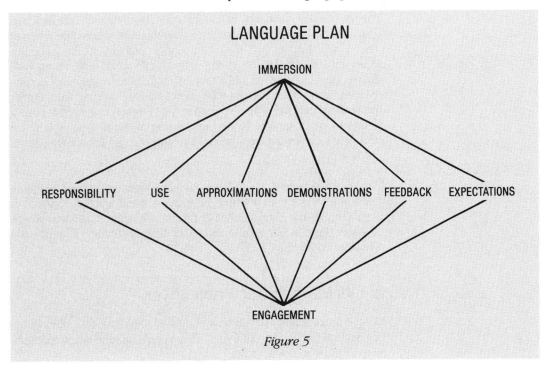

Figure 5

This plan emphasised the **immersion** dimension of natural learning. In this plan, the notion of immersion permeates the whole classroom context and filters down through everything which happens. Such a plan necessitates the accumulation of books and texts of all kinds, genre, content and levels.

The second line of this plan deals mainly with the behaviours of the teacher and the learners. One side of the rhombus deals predominantly with teacher behaviour. It is mainly the teacher who **demonstrates**, sets the **expectations** and **responds**. The other side of the rhombus deals predominantly with the learner's behaviour. The learners **use** (employ, practise); they continually **approximate** (have a go); they are also required to take **responsibility** for deciding about what to learn, what to engage with, in what order to approach any given set of tasks and how to go about any particular task. The third line highlights the necessity for **engagement**. Just as **immersion** permeates the whole classroom from the top of the rhombus, the necessity for **engagement** underlies the whole plan, guiding and influencing all of the teacher's actions and interactions with the learners. None of what occurs in the top section of the plan is of much use unless some engagement on the part of the learners is also taking place.

As this kind of classroom gathers momentum, the demarcation boundaries between the roles of teacher and learner become blurred. The teacher demonstrates, expects, responds — but so do the learners, especially in their many interactions with each other. The roles of teacher and learner will shift from one interaction to the next. For example, a child may be in the learner role when interacting with the teacher, and one minute after ending that exchange may become teacher for another learner who seeks help or advice. Conversely, the teacher may become the learner when the class expert on using ferrets to catch rabbits begins explaining in detail how it is done in a piece of writing he's brought to the teacher for sharing or an opinion.

This is only one version of a language plan. There are others. Teachers intending to move to a whole language/natural learning classroom need to take the time to devise one which suits them and which captures the essence of the model of learning which is explained in earlier chapters.

B. Deciding literacy objectives

Most educational enterprises are guided by aims and objectives. Literacy education is no different. There comes a time when teachers have to ask questions such as:
— What is it that we are trying to achieve with respect to reading and writing in our classrooms?
— With respect to literacy, what kinds of learners do we wish to emerge from our classrooms when we've finished with them?
— What is it that we wish our charges to be able to do as readers and writers?

These are basic questions about aims and objectives. There have been many attempts to provide answers for such questions. Those I have seen over the years range from lists of separate skills (sometimes numbering in the hundreds), to lists of objectives for each specific class, grade or age level in the school, to rather vague collections of statements about 'reading and writing for different purposes'. I have never found these approaches to be very useful and/or satisfying.

I used to wonder why. I've come to realise that a holistic approach to language requires a holistic approach to aims and objectives in language education. Just as one should not fragment language into what appear to be logical sets of sub-skills and sub-concepts, nor should one try to fragment one's aims and objectives into 'stages' or 'class levels' or sets of so-called 'specific aims'. Rather, we need to sort out some very general aims and then arrange our classrooms so that the probability that these general aims will be attained is maximised. Whatever aims we devise, they are a function of what we know, value and believe about reading, writing and learning in our culture. Consequently, aims and objectives can never be fixed and immutable. As our values and levels of knowledge change, so will our aims and objectives.

Here are some very general aims which I hold about teaching reading and writing. I want to stress that these are personal and idiosyncratic to me. There is nothing sacrosanct or inviolate about them. I offer them only as an example/model from which others might like to work.

★ I would aim to help learners become aware of, and understand, the power of reading and writing. I would especially aim to make them consciously aware of the potential of reading and writing as a means of developing both learning and thinking and as a means of modifying, creating and extending learning and thought.

Reason: Our culture values and rewards those who learn and think. Learning and thinking are enhanced through control of language forms. Reading and writing lead to control of language forms, especially if learners are consciously aware of how the two activities support and extend each other.

★ I would aim to produce graduates who are confident about their abilities to use reading and writing for a whole range of learning and thinking tasks.

Reason: Learning is enhanced if learners are confident about their ability to learn.

★ I would aim to produce graduates who would continue to read and write long after formal instruction had finished.

Reason: Once learned, the skills of literacy ought to be durable — the probability of such skills enduring is increased if learners are positive about them. Effective learning is facilitated if the learner has positive attitudes towards what is being learned.

These are very general aims and apply across the whole literacy learning spectrum from beginners to higher levels of schooling. Typically they lead to more specific aims. The nature of these specific aims will vary from teacher to teacher. Furthermore, as teachers learn more about language, they will change the nature of their aims.

For example, one teacher whose work I've monitored carefully over four years began with two sets of specific aims, one set for reading and one for writing.

LANGUAGE EVALUATION SHEET - Reading

Name **Zaklina K**

✓	Shows obvious enjoyment and displays a willing attitude towards reading.
✓	Borrows books regularly from the school library.
✓	Can talk about reading and the reading process.
✓	Reads for a sustained period of time.
✓	Knows how to choose a book suited to his/her needs and interests.
✓	Applies strategies to overcome reader's block.
✓	Recognises good and bad miscues.
✓	Predicts meanings in text by appropriate use of cues (grapho-phonic, semantic, syntactic)
✓	Selects literature appropriate to his/her reading ability.
✓	Understands the value of re-reading parts for information.
	Can skim read to obtain information.
✓	Can handle longer texts.
✓	Shows developing reference skills.
	Can summarise including all major points.
✓	Selects reading material appropriate to his/her reading ability.
✓	Selects a wide range of literature to read.
✓	Can describe storyline development in particular novels: setting, problem, climax, ending, in order.
✓	Can identify characters and character traits.
✓	Can classify books: fiction, non-fiction, fantasy, etc.

LANGUAGE EVALUATION SHEET - *Writing*

Name **Zaklina K**

✓	Displays a willing attitude towards writing.
✓	Willingly seeks and accepts advice.
	Attempts a variety of genre.
✓	Able to gather/brainstorm for information.
✓	Can select a topic.
✓	Makes a positive attempt to edit to the limit of his/her maturity.
✓	Is showing organisation towards story form (beginning, middle & end).
	Is consulting a variety of sources in search of information.
	Writes leads that arouse interest.
	Writes descriptively and gives details.
✓	Reveals a growing vocabulary.
✓	Sequences ideas logically.
	Writes satisfactory endings.
✓	Shows improved control of spelling.
✓	Displays word attack skills.
	Structures sentences correctly.
✓	a) simple punctuation
	b) commas
✓	c) question sentence
✓	d) speech marks
	Structures a paragraph using a topic sentence.

Two years later, as she learned more about the relationship between reading and writing, she merged them into a set of 'expectations' which looked like this:

* Positive attitudes towards learning.

* Seeking/accepting advice willingly.

* Accepting responsibility for learning and organisation.

* Accepting mistakes as a natural part of learning.

* Having confidence to discuss learning.

* Accepting the necessity for justifications in discussion & argument.

* Control of a variety of genre in reading, writing and speaking.

* Making considered decisions with regard to reading, writing & speaking.

* Understanding the need for preparedness/correctness when going public.

* Consulting a variety of sources in search of information.

* Reading for a sustained period of time.

* Recognizing good/bad miscues.

* Having strategies to overcome blocks in reading/writing.

* Understanding the value of re-reading for information.

* Making a positive attempt to edit.

* Displaying a developing vocabulary.

* Controlling the conventions of writing.

* Understanding the elements of various forms of writing.

* Applying knowledge.

She'll probably change again in the future.

I am prepared to argue that if these broad aims are achieved, the sets of smaller, sub-aims which teachers have traditionally worried about will be taken care of as a consequence. It's a kind of 'Look after the dollars and the cents will look after themselves' philosophy.

Attaining these aims is contingent upon what teachers know about reading, writing and learning. Those who have the most understanding of how reading, writing and learning work and relate to each other have the best chance to organise their classrooms so that very general aims like those described above will be attained.

2. Making Decisions about How the Programme Will be Run

A. Organising time

The label 'whole language' describes an approach to language teaching which insists that language acts are not fragmented for the purposes of learning. One of the corollaries of this stance is that time cannot be fragmented either. Because many teachers have spent most of their professional lives measuring time in fifteen- or thirty-minute blocks while they teach fragments of language (the thirty-minute grammar lesson), some will experience difficulty with this notion. It's a difficult one to explain. I've always found it easiest to describe how other teachers have resolved the problem. Here's one method of organising time which I've seen in a number of classrooms and which I know works.

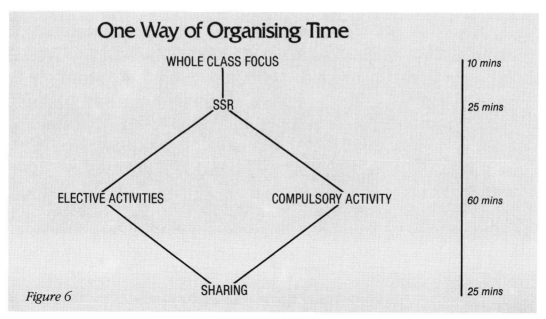

One Way of Organising Time

WHOLE CLASS FOCUS — 10 mins

SSR — 25 mins

ELECTIVE ACTIVITIES   COMPULSORY ACTIVITY — 60 mins

SHARING — 25 mins

Figure 6

This time line represents the first two hours of the school day. On the teacher's timetable it is represented by the label 'Language'. It can be seen from the figure above that the time has been organised by the teacher around four descriptive labels. These labels represent what the learners and teacher do during these periods of time:

(i) Whole Class Focus Time
(ii) Sustained Silent Reading Time
(iii) Activity Time — elective activity/compulsory activity
(iv) Sharing Time

Let me describe briefly what happens in each of these broad time slots.

(i) Whole Class Focus Time

This is essentially a time when the teacher has the whole group together. It is used to:

— focus learners' attention on tasks, events and organisational or housekeeping matters;
— demonstrate an infinite range of literacy-related skills, knowledge and attitudes that learners need to engage with and learn;
— communicate teacher expectations about each individual learner and about the class as a group of learners. There is also the opportunity to communicate expectations about how enjoyable, useful, relevant and functional reading and writing can be.

Teacher reading: a powerful demonstration of the language of texts, of how reading 'works', and what reading can be used for.

The teachers whom I've observed over the last few years typically spend a minute or two dealing with housekeeping matters (if there are any) and then they will:

— read to the class, **or**
— write in front of the class, usually thinking out loud as they do so, **or**
— demonstrate how new language activities are done, e.g., how a literary sociogram or story grammar is done.

The specific details will, of course, vary from class to class and age group to age group.

What happens if teachers decide to read during whole class focus time?

Teachers of younger children, if they decide to read, usually follow some variation of the well-known shared book format. Teachers of older children usually read in serial form from children's literature. These reading times have the following characteristics:

— Typically they are for **enjoyment**. At least this is what is communicated to the children. There are no comprehension quizzes ('Now, who can remember the name of the little girl in the story?'); there is no serious study of the text ('Let's look at these words in the story — what do you think they mean?'); there is no 'over-dwelling' on some trivial aspect of the text (interrupting the flow of the story to teach some point which emerges from the text).

— Typically these sessions involve **retelling** and **predicting**. They always begin with a recount to the stage of the story that has been reached and some predictions of what the children think might happen next.

— Typically the teacher **interrupts** the flow of reading. This isn't a time when the teacher simply reads and the children listen. The interruptions are, however, minimal and they serve a very special purpose — to bring to the conscious awareness of the listeners some aspect of how texts are structured, used, or processed. For example:

> *Did you notice how E. B. White uses detail in his description of the barn just here? You might like to consider that in your own writing.*

or

> *Roald Dahl has used another character similar to this in another story. Does he sound familiar?*

If the children are very young or immature from a literacy point of view, the interruption might focus on something less sophisticated, such as:

> *Oh, here's a word I've never seen before. I'll just say 'something' and go on — perhaps I'll work out what it means later.*

Such interruptions are always followed by an immediate return to the story.

— Typically, at the conclusion of the teacher's reading there is a brief discussion of what's been read. This discussion focuses on the **listeners'** responses to what's been heard and the meanings it held for **them**. If the text is being read as a serial, there are usually some further predictions made. Again there is no comprehension quiz.

Some teachers of very young children sometimes use this period to take their young readers on a 'print walk'. This involves walking around the school or the room finding print which can be read and having it read by an 'expert' (the teacher, another child, a parent), or perhaps even reading it in unison as the 'expert' points to it.

What happens if teachers decide to write during whole class focus time?

If the teacher decides to write during this period, she typically demonstrates and 'loud thinks' a text on the chalkboard or overhead projector.

> *'I want you to watch and listen while I show you how I write a notice to parents about the swimming carnival.'*

or

> *'I'm going to share this rough draft of what I wrote last night. It's a poem about peace that I've been working on. I've copied it onto an overhead transparency so you can see exactly what I did and I'll tell you why I did certain things.'*

Again, there is no 'over-dwelling' or direct teaching. Instead there is open sharing of a process or artifact (demonstration) and a covert communication of attitude or expectation. A variation of this is to use somebody else's writing as a demonstration of how writing is done. For example:

> *Remember I read* **'Charlotte's Web'** *to you last month? Well, here's a piece of writing from chapter three of that book. Remember when E. B. White describes the barn? I said then that I thought it was pretty good writing. Well, I still do. It's excellent writing. I've photocopied the first couple of paragraphs of that chapter. Let's read it silently and see if we can work out why this piece of writing is so good.'*

A frequent comment made by both teachers and children whom I've interviewed about this period of their language sessions is that 'the time goes so quickly'. However, it should be understood that whole class focus organisation does not have to be restricted to the beginning of the session. It is legitimate to call the class together at other times during the language session.

(ii) Sustained Silent Reading (SSR) Time

This is a well-known teaching practice. It involves learners being free to select and read or peruse any book or text from those which are available in the classroom. While the rules may vary from class to class and from age level to age level, there are a few simple ones which seem to be common:

Firstly, everyone must select a book, sit somewhere quietly and appear to be interacting with the book in some way.

Secondly, it is a quiet time; no one is allowed to talk about or share what they're reading. There will be time for that later.

Thirdly, books cannot be changed until a certain minimal time period has elapsed, so choices should be made carefully.

Fourthly, as there will be a sharing time later, readers should be reading or perusing in a way that will enable them to share something from what they've read.

Finally, any adults in the room should be seen to be reading silently as well.

Everyone must select a book, sit somewhere quietly and appear to be interacting with the book in some way.

Often when I describe SSR to teachers at workshops, many will comment:

> *That's all very well for children who can already read, Brian, but I teach Kindergarten and they could never do that.'*

I try to explain that just as learners exhibit different degrees of control over the spoken form of language, so they will exhibit different degrees of control over the written form. Just as we don't prevent immature talkers from engaging in talk or dialogue, neither should we prevent immature readers or writers from indulging in reading or writing.

For purposes of very immature readers and writers I'm prepared to stretch the definition of reading and writing to include 'reading-like behaviour' or 'writing-like behaviour'. I'm also willing to reduce the time for SSR from twenty-five minutes to ten minutes. Under these conditions it is possible for so-called 'non-readers' to take part in SSR sessions, provided there are texts available with which such immature learners can engage. If teachers of very immature readers are still unconvinced about the feasibility of this, I share with them some of the kinds of 'reading' behaviour which I've observed when immature readers have been expected to participate in SSR sessions.

'Reading-like' Behaviours of Very Young Children Observed in a Whole Language Kindergarten

1. Recreating text from memory, turning pages randomly.

2. Recreating a text from the pictures only. Each picture represents a complete text — no continuity of story line.

3. As above, with continuous story line which may or may not match the text in the book.

4. Recreating text from memory, running eyes and/or finger over text but not one-to-one matching of print with meaning.

5. Just turning pages, frontwards and backwards, but obviously engaging with pictures.

6. Sitting next to someone else engaged in 1-5, and sometimes collaborating and/or intervening in the other's reading-like behaviour.

(iii) Activity Time

This is that period of the language session when learners must:

★ make choices and accept responsibility for them (**responsibility**);
★ practise and employ their developing language skills (**use**);

★ have a go and share their immature attempts at using reading and writing (**approximation**);

★ teach and learn from their peers (**demonstrate for** others, **engage with** the demonstrations of others);

★ listen to and comment on others' attempts to read and write (**respond**).

This is a time when teachers:

★ **demonstrate** a whole range of literacy-related knowledge, attitudes and processes;

★ communicate and define their **expectations** about learners and their learning;

★ **respond** and give **feedback** to learners' attempts to use reading and writing.

During activity time, teachers can hit base with small groups.

During this busy time teachers observe, evaluate, interact, teach, redirect, refocus, demand, pursue, question, clarify, analyse, support, celebrate, coerce, coax, cajole, sympathise and empathise. In the time line shown in figure 6 on page 89 this period lasts for one hour of a two-hour session. While the length of this period will vary from class to class and from age level to age level, its **relative** length will probably remain constant, i.e. about 50% of the total time allocated for any one language session.

The following is what typically happens in this part of the session: The learners are expected to work on any one of a group of reading/writing activities which the teacher has previously prepared.

There are two kinds of activities — elective and compulsory. Elective activities are just that — learners are free to choose what they will do from a range of options. Compulsory activities are those that are chosen by the teacher. While the majority of the class make moves to begin their elective activities, the teacher introduces the compulsory activity to one small group of children. (On Mondays it's her Monday Group, on Tuesdays it's her Tuesday Group and so on.) Once the compulsory group has begun its compulsory activity the teacher begins to rove, interacting with pupils about their work.

To the untrained eye, the scene in the classroom would look a little disorganised. Groups of children talking, arguing, browsing, writing and moving from the reference section of the class library back to the fiction section. Others reading from rough drafts to peers, others talking to the teacher and others just reading silently. Amid all this activity the teacher moves from group to group or child to child, talking, questioning, responding and then moving on.

Groups of children talking, arguing, browsing, writing and moving.

(iv) Sharing Time

This is the final segment of time in the language session. It is the culmination of the two hours of reading, writing, talking and listening. Now, learners in the group get a chance to verbalise their responses to what they've read or to get responses from their peers on what they've written. Those who don't share, get the opportunity to listen, respond and reflect upon what their peers think, the kinds of problems they have, the kind of language they use to talk about these things. Now they are able to question their peers about what they've read or written or how they've solved problems.

Learners in the group get a chance to verbalise their responses.

During this time teachers can very subtly model how questions can be asked or answered.

It's a time when teachers can draw to the conscious awareness of the learners an almost infinite range of connections between the content and characters of books, the structures and shapes of texts, the processes involved in reading and writing and other accoutrements of literacy.

Above all, it's a time when a great deal of learning, teaching and evaluating can take place.

The precise form which this sharing time takes will vary. The most successful sharing times I've seen over the last few years have a few basic ground rules:

★ **Sharing is a voluntary activity.** While the expectation is that during the school year a minimum number of turns to share will be taken, just when those turns are taken is left to each child to decide. Talking in front of an audience can be a threatening experience until you feel comfortable with the audience and the whole process of sharing.

★ **Comments and questions must not be nasty or hurtful.** It is legitimate to question and seek clarification and even disagree with another's interpretation if this is done in a way which preserves another's dignity.

★ **Only one person at a time may hold the floor.**

B. Organising space

In order to use time in ways similar to that already described, one needs to organise space as well. Whole language/natural learning classrooms are characterised by learner movement and learner interaction, periods when the class becomes a single group with a single purpose and periods when the class becomes a series of discrete groups with a multiplicity of different purposes.

The desks are set out so that children can move easily and talk to each other.

Classrooms which operate this way obviously need desks and furniture arranged so that the movement, interaction, group work, individual work, quiet times and whole class focus times are made possible. The desks are set out so that children can move easily and talk to each other. A chalk board stands where the whole class can see it. Resources and materials are arranged so that children have ready access to them.

Figure 7 shows one teacher's plan for organising a classroom so that these spaces can be created for 25-30 pupils.

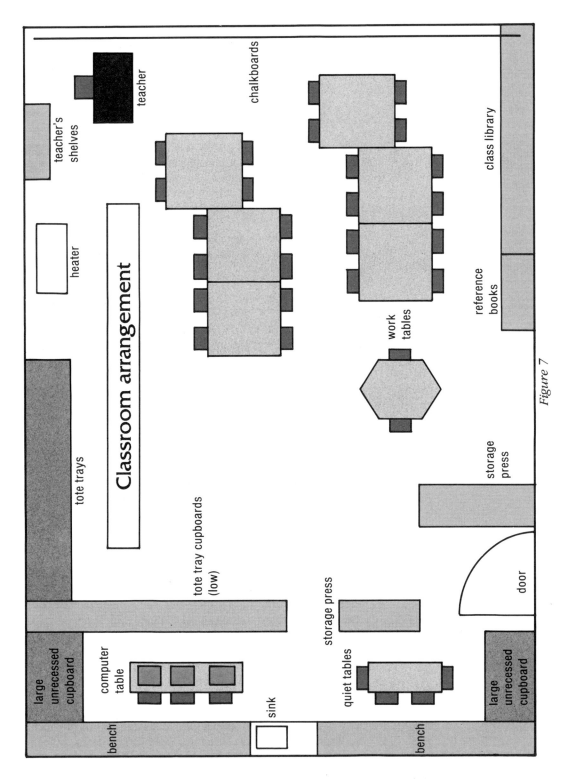

Classroom arrangement

teacher

teacher's shelves

chalkboards

heater

class library

tote trays

reference books

work tables

storage press

tote tray cupboards (low)

large unrecessed cupboard

computer table

storage press

quiet tables

door

sink

large unrecessed cupboard

bench

bench

Figure 7

Such a space plan does not require an extraordinarily large room. I've witnessed such space created in average-sized rooms which have been crowded with cupboards and other furniture. Anyone, with a little planning, can create the spaces which are needed.

C. Organising resources

Both written and oral texts are the tools of trade in a whole language classroom. They are what the learners are immersed in and the source of most of the demonstrations of how both forms of the language are used and structured. Because they are part of the social interactions which are constantly occurring in classrooms, oral texts do not have to be collected nor do they have to be stored for future use. They are easily and readily generated in the ebb and flow of classroom talk. Because they are ephemeral it is difficult to store them, although audiotape is a possibility.

Written texts are different. They are more tangible and cannot be generated as easily. If written texts are to be constantly used and therefore learned about they need to be collected and stored. The collection of sufficient, suitable written texts is the major resource problem for the whole language/natural learning classroom.

Just as the oral language learner needed to be saturated by the medium he was trying to learn to control in order to tease out how the various systems of language all worked to make meaning, so the learner who is trying to gain control over the written form needs to be immersed in the medium from which he can infer how the written form of the language works — print! This means books, magazines, newspapers, wall charts. Following are some general principles I've learned about creating and using resources from the teachers I've observed over the years.

Create a library in your room

★ Ask the school librarian to allow the learners in your class to select two or three books each that they'd like to have in the classroom for an extended period of time.

★ Bulk borrow poetry books, picture books, collections of short stories.

★ Beg, borrow or scrounge non-fiction texts and magazines.

★ Have as wide a range of textual forms available as possible. Include predictable and familiar structures such as fairy tales, fables and limericks.

★ Find authors who write for a range of ability levels so that less able and more able readers can share common authors. This makes it possible for Peter, whose reading skills are not highly developed, to talk about Robin Klein as an author with Melissa, who is virtually an adult reader. (Robin Klein is an author who writes for a wide range of readers.)

★ Try to build up collections which feature different works by the same author. Learners develop tastes for certain authors and will devour all the books that any one author has written once this taste begins to develop.

Flood the room with useful wall charts

★ Put songs, poems and chants onto charts and read them together frequently.

★ Children's science experiments, social science reports, observations and other child-generated writing can be put onto charts, displayed and used frequently.

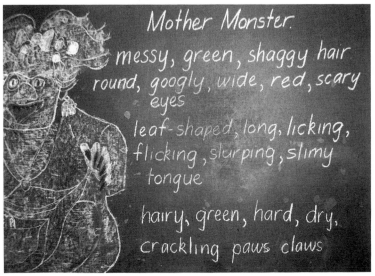

★ Reference charts should be made and often referred to, for example:
   ● birthday charts,
   ● weather charts,
   ● charts of synonyms, metaphors, similes, problem words,
   ● charts of good leads, written by other children or found in other texts,
   ● summaries of discoveries about texts, e.g. characteristics of fairy tales, fables, etc. (see examples on page 139)
   ● charts which contain samples of class members' published texts,
   ● charts which summarise class contracts, rules, expectations.

Such resources, even the most carefully made and colourful, are of little use unless the learners regularly engage with and use them.

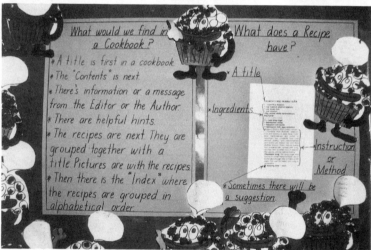

D. Demonstrations

Teachers have a two-fold responsibility with respect to demonstrations. Firstly, they have to give them. Secondly, they have to draw the attention of the learners to the demonstrations which other persons or other artifacts provide.

The demonstrations which young children receive from their 'teachers' (mothers, fathers, grandparents, siblings, neighbours) when they are learning to talk are easy to describe. People simply use oral language in front of learner talkers and gradually they learn to talk. It is tempting to try to argue that with respect to literacy, a parallel situation should be possible. That is, people should merely read, write, spell or engage in other kinds of literacy behaviour in front of learners and they will learn to read and write. While the underlying principles might be the same, there are two reasons why the demonstrations given by teachers in the literacy classroom need to be a little different.

1) There is not the same amount of time available. The time dimension of learning to talk cannot be replicated for the learning to read/write/spell situation. Because the same **quantity** of demonstrations cannot be supplied, the **quality** of the demonstrations which are given must be high.

2) With respect to the written form of language, the degree to which the learner must be consciously aware of the way in which it works (what I have been calling **meta-textual awareness**) needs to be greater.

In the classrooms in which I've been observing, teachers try to accommodate these two differences in a number of ways. They try to provide as many demonstrations as possible of literacy behaviour by doing lots of reading and writing in front of their students. During as many of these demonstrations as possible they think out loud. A variation of this is to talk about the thinking and doing processes that someone must have gone through in order to produce a certain kind of literacy product, say, a piece of writing — what might be labelled a retrospective 'think-aloud'.

In whole language classrooms, teachers are continually demonstrating how reading, writing and thinking are done.

103

Combining thinking out loud and talking about with the actual demonstrations of **doing** reading and writing helps learners make many of the conscious connections between the oral and written forms of the language which need to be made. Let me demonstrate what I mean with a couple of examples. (Pun intended.)

EXAMPLE 1: A think-aloud demonstration for very young learners

Scene: A typical whole language/natural learning kindergarten classroom. Over thirty children between four-and-a-half and five-and-a-half years of age. The room is filled with teacher-made charts and some child-made charts. The teacher has an overhead projector and some blank acetates ready at the front of the room. The children are accustomed to being called together as a group for some whole class focus time several times a day. Often they read through some of the charts with the teacher. Today she calls them together as a whole class and this is what transpires:

Teacher: "I want you all to watch me and listen to what I say. I'm going to show you how I go about writing a story. While I do it I'm going to talk to myself and think out loud so you'll all get some ideas on how grown-ups write things like stories. While I'm talking to myself, I'll ask myself lots of questions and I'll answer them. I don't want you to answer them this time. You think you understand?"

Class: A chorus of "Yes, Miss", "Uh-huh" and head nodding, etc.

Teacher: "I want to write a story that other kindergarten children will like to read. Let me see, what kinds of stories do kindergarten children like to read?" (Looks thoughtful for a few seconds.) "I know, they like to read stories about what happens to other people. Now, let me see, what's happened to me lately that would make a good story . . ." (Looks thoughtful again, as if recalling. Suddenly, she looks bright and eager as if a brilliant idea has just occurred to her.) "I know, last Thursday was late-night shopping for our town and I was running late. It was getting close to the time when the supermarket closed and I had to get a lot of things, so I rushed into the store, grabbed a trolley from the trolley depot and hurried along the aisles. Now, I got one of those trolleys that has a wonky wheel, you know, that goes up and down and is hard to steer?"

Class: A chorus of "Yes, Miss", "Uh-huh" and nodding of heads.

Teacher: "Well, I hurried along the aisles getting the things I needed for cooking and eating and I came to the place where eggs are kept. Now, I needed about four packets of eggs, so I began to load them onto the groceries I already had on the trolley. Then I went to push the whole lot up to the check-out lady when the wheel started bumping up and down, the trolley started wriggling from one side to the other . . . and guess what? The eggs fell off and spilled all over the floor and made a terrible mess and I was so embarrassed and the poor store supervisor had to get one of the juniors to get a mop and bucket and clean it all up. I was really embarrassed and felt bad about it all. I'll write about that event."

Having reached this point, the teacher moves towards the overhead projector (OHP) or the chalkboard and signals that she is going to begin writing.

Teacher: (As if thinking to herself, rubbing chin, staring into space.) "Now, let me think, how should I start a story like that? I know, I'll say the first few sentences first, just to get them clear in my head. 'Last Thursday night I went shopping. I was in a hurry and just grabbed the first trolley which was available. That was the first mistake I made.' Yes, that sounds good, I'll say the rest later when I get this bit written."

The teacher then moves to the OHP with pen poised.

Teacher: "Now, what's the first sentence again? 'Last Thursday night I went shopping.' 'Last' is the first word I want to write. How do I write 'last' when I'm in kindergarten? Oh, there it is on the weather chart. I'll just copy it down, l/a/s/t. Now, 'Thursday'. How am I going to write 'Thursday'? Oh, there it is on the days of the week chart that we read now and then. I'll copy it down."

Imagine the teacher working through each word in the first sentence like this until she comes to 'shopping'. If shopping is not on a chart somewhere in the room, this is what could possibly happen:

Teacher: "Now I'm up to 'shopping'. How am I going to write 'shopping'? It's not on any of the charts around the room. I know, I'll try to sound it out. Let me see if I can say it really slowly and hear the sounds in it. Sh-o-p-ing. What's the first sound I can hear? Sh — sh. How do you write sh? I know that starts Shelley's name and Shane's name. I'll look at their names and see if I can work it out."

What has been demonstrated in this little, five-minute scene? I would argue that a great deal is being made available to the learners who witnessed it. Among other things I would argue that the following have been demonstrated about literacy.

★ Stories which are drawn from personal experience are a good starting point for beginning one's writing career.

★ Other kindergarten children like stories which have details about real happenings in them.

★ Composing orally precedes writing anything down.

★ When one is in kindergarten and has not yet solved the written language puzzle, there is a range of strategies one can bring to bear to help in getting the task done, including scrounging from around the room and sounding out.

★ What is meant by the concepts 'word', 'sentence', 'sound' (i.e. syllable), 'letter', and a few letter names (l/a/s/t).

★ The fact that words can be broken into syllables and how it is done.

★ How letters are made, how print goes across the page from left to right, how there are spaces between words and a host of other basics about literacy.

EXAMPLE 2: A think-aloud demonstration for older learners

Scene: A Grade 5 class of thirty or so children, arranged in whole class focus position. The teacher is about to begin reading as a serial the story 'Hating Alison Ashley' by Robin Klein. Earlier in the year the children have had another Klein book read to them as a serial.

> **Teacher:** "I'm going to read another of Robin Klein's books to you. It's called 'Hating Alison Ashley'. Now, Robin Klein has written lots of other children's books . . ." (Here she stops talking to the group and begins to engage in behaviour which could be called talking to oneself or thinking aloud.) "Let me see, just how many other books has she had published? I'll just look through the details of authors which publishers often put in the front of books. Ah, here it is . . ."

Anyone watching this scene would probably say that at this point the teacher's behaviour changes and it becomes obvious that she's stopped talking to herself and is now talking to the class again.

> **Teacher:** "Yes, here it is, a whole list of books by Robin Klein and the dates when they were published. I'll read them out and you mentally tick off any that you've already read."

What is being demonstrated in this little, two-minute scene? Again, I would argue quite a lot, including:

★ the fact that books often include an author's 'previously published' list,

★ that often the dates of these other publications are also given,

★ that this information can sometimes supply details about the way in which the book fits into a series (as with the C S Lewis 'Narnia' series or the Roald Dahl sequences) — often this material is essential for fully understanding a book,

★ where one usually finds such details — somewhere near the front, before the body of the text actually begins.

EXAMPLE 3: A 'talk about' or retrospective 'think aloud' for older learners

Scene: A class of thirty or so Grade 5 children. On a previous day, the teacher had demonstrated how to brainstorm for a topic and had come up with a topic which he said he was going to try to write about. It was called 'The Day I Found the Body' and was essentially a recount of an event from his own school days. (He'd truanted school, gone to the beach and found a body floating in the surf. He was interviewed by a news reporter and his picture appeared in the evening newspaper that his father always bought.) The teacher had promised to write a draft that night and bring it in to share. He has made photocopies of his draft and hands them out.

The Day I Found the Body

By Brian Cambourne

DRAFT 1

I remember it as if it were yesterday although it happened over 30 years ago. A Thursday in May, one of those calm autumn days that I enjoyed so much. I was walking to school thinking about how dull and boring it was going to be; I was in a bad mood, because my mother had yelled at me for being slow at getting dressed and my big sister had yelled at me for staying in the bathroom too long. The night before my Dad had

yelled at me for breaking the switch on his ^new soldering iron. I also know that ~~it~~ when I got to school the teacher would yell at me too because we'd be doing fractions and I was hopeless at them. ~~I could hear him~~
As I trudged to school I could hear him in my head
"Well Cambourne, what's your answer, eh?" When I gave my answer, (which I knew would be wrong) he would say "I don't know Cambourne, you must have been kicked in the head by a moth at birth; can't you learn anything?"
Then the whole class would laugh and I'd sink (further) into my seat, trying to hide my red face and (embarrassment) No wonder I felt in a bad mood!

Now, in order to get to the ~~school~~ ~~beach~~ school gate I had to walk up a hill which overlooked the beach which was near my school. I loved the beach and spent all of my spare time there. I knew every rockpool, every current and rip, and felt I knew every grain of sand.

It was a place where I always felt happy.
On this particular day as I |got to| reached ? the top of the hill the beach caught my eye. It looked really beautiful. ~~Because~~ it was autumn and a weekday, not many people were there.
The waves were just my size, the tide was just right; I made a quick decision. I would wag school, and have fun at the beach — that would be better than doing dumb fractions and being laughed at
I turned toward the beach and away from school.
Little did I know what I was letting myself in for.

Teacher: "Well, here's the draft I promised you. I didn't get too far. That's what happens when you write. You seem to get so far and then you get blocked or run out of ideas and you need help. The best help comes from other authors who understand the problems you're going through, so, I'm sharing my draft with you. I need some response from other authors. What do you think?"

108

There is a pause while the class reads through the draft.

> **Bruno:** "I really like that bit about where your dad yells at you and your mum and sister yelled at you. That happens to me, too."
>
> **Spodra:** "Yeah, and I like that bit about the beach. I feel like that about the beach too. But why did you put the circle around 'embarrassment'?"
>
> **Teacher:** "I'm glad you asked that. It's just something I do to help me. I'm not sure how that word is spelled — but I didn't want to stop composing and go off to the dictionary to look it up because my ideas were really coming then and I knew they'd just dry up if I stopped. So that circle is a sign to remind me that I need to check the spelling of that word before I start a public draft."

Similar questions were asked about other marks the teacher had used on his draft. What is being demonstrated here? Again, a multiplicity of facts and processes, including:

★ how drafts look (messy, with lots of crossings out and changes),

★ that composition is more important than accurate spelling at the drafting stage,

★ that it's normal for authors to run out of ideas and to seek help,

★ that drafts are malleable,

★ how words are spelled, sentences punctuated and stories are structured,

★ what readers like and respond to.

This kind of demonstration can be replicated with writing from the authors whom the children are reading or having read to them, e.g. the excerpt from *Charlotte's Web* described earlier. There is no limit to the range and variety of demonstrations about how reading, writing and all of the different facets of literacy can be done.

It is important to remember that non-narrative texts can also be demonstrated in exactly the same way. Similar kinds of demonstrations can be supplied if teachers are interested in children learning to control the different forms that reports or instructional prose take, or that argument or persuasive writing take, or any of the many kinds of writing which are possible.

E. Developing activities

The activities which teachers provide for learners to do during language sessions serve some extremely important functions in the whole language classroom. Among other things they provide:

a) the medium for learners to **use** (practise, employ) their developing language skills and knowledge,

b) an arena for learners and teachers to interact and focus on an infinite range of literacy concepts and skills at the level of individual need,

c) the medium for much of the evaluation and monitoring which teachers do,

d) many of the links between reading, writing, talking and listening of which learners need to become conscious,

e) the teacher with a form of control over her programme — the activities she devises enable her to include and/or exclude whatever concepts, skills, processes, knowledge she thinks are appropriate,

f) an arena for relevant learning. Learners who are intent on finishing or completing an activity which they think is worthwhile are more likely to engage with demonstrations or feedback about the skills and/or knowledge they need to use, than if they are engaged on a 'dummy' or contrived task.

In order for the activities to provide these functions, they need to be carefully designed and/or chosen. Teachers should not think that any kinds of 'seatwork' or stencil work are sufficient. My observations over the years have convinced me that the activities which teachers either design or select for learners to complete during activity time are crucial factors in maximising the probability that the general aims described above will be achieved. There are four basic requirements that language activities used in whole language classrooms should possess.

1. They should be activities which coerce learners into using language as a means to achieve an end other than learning about the language. In other words, control over the various forms of language emerges as if it was an incidental by-product of using the language for broader purposes. The teacher, of course, has planned that the seemingly 'incidental' learning will take place. While learners, typically, are not consciously aware that they are doing the activities in order to learn to control specific aspects of the written language, the climate in which they are operating is one which encourages them to reflect upon what they are learning.

2. They should be activities which cannot be successfully completed without interacting with others.

3. They should be activities which necessitate reading, writing, talking, listening and being maximally involved each time.

4. The resources for completing these activities should all be available and readily accessible in the classroom.

The time line on page 89 shows that two kinds of activities are carried out in activity time — namely, **elective** and **compulsory**. Both kinds of activities should meet the four basic requirements I have just listed. The difference between an 'elective' and a 'compulsory' activity is to be found in who decides whether it will be done, not in the kind of activity it actually is.

There is no definitive and/or exhaustive list of activities' that can be drawn up and presented to teachers. The potential list is infinite. Here are some activities which I've observed teachers use. They are offered only for purposes of illustration. They are definitely not intended to be a recommended set which all teachers of all grades should use.

Continued Silent Reading

On the time line on page 89, Activity Time follows immediately after silent reading time. One of the activities which children may choose as an elective activity is to continue reading. It seems artificial and contrived to cease reading a book with which one is deeply engaged to take up some other activity just because it's a certain time of day. Sometimes the concession of shared reading is allowed as a related option — two readers may read the same text and talk about it as they read.

Writing/Process Writing

Just as it is contrived to stop reading because of the time of day, it is equally as contrived to have a separate writing time. Most of the activities which follow on from, or flow out of, silent reading time will have a writing component to them if designed according to the preceding criteria. Furthermore, many of the demonstrations given during different times of the language session are of writing and writing procedures, techniques, conventions and so on. Writing in the sense of constructing texts of different genre for different purposes therefore becomes one of the elective options available during activity time. For example, part of the class contract might be to complete to publication stage three pieces of writing. One narrative, one report and one procedural (how to) text.

Conferring/Discussing/Seeking Peer Help

In some classrooms it is mandatory that learners who need help with any activity or task which they've undertaken should first seek it from peers in the classroom. Thus, 'conferencing' is a possible elective activity but depends upon an activity having been already commenced.

Peers are useful resources when solving language problems.

Complete a 'Language Activity' Card

Some teachers devise a set of language activity cards which are kept filed in the room. Learners are free to select from this file any activity they like. Many of the activities on these cards can be applied to the book or books which were read during silent reading time. Thus they are activities which can be applied again and again to the different books which children read. Here are some of the many I've seen used:

★ character analysis of characters appearing in books read,
★ summarising book plots ('Write a blurb and illustrate it'),
★ completing a literacy sociogram,
★ doing a story grammar,
★ doing a retelling of a specially selected text,
★ sequencing a cut-up text.

For further suggestions, see Johnson and Louis *(1985)* and Brown and Cambourne *(1987)*.

Weekly General Knowledge Sheets

These sheets are designed to coerce the use of all kinds of reference books, such as dictionaries, thesauruses, encyclopaedias and atlases; see the following sample.

GENERAL KNOWLEDGE QUIZ

Name _____

1. Name 2 things gulls may show aggression over:

    _____   _____

2. What is the average lifetime of the African elephant?

    _____

3. Of which countries are these the capital cities?

    a) Santiago _____   e) Rome _____

    b) Canberra _____   f) Copenhagen _____

    c) Washington _____   g) Athens _____

    d) Paris _____   h) Rangoon _____

4. Who is the author of 'Captain Beaky'?

    _____

5. What purpose has the glossary in a book?

    _____

6. In what part of the newspaper would you find the sports pages?

    _____

7. What kind of author is a journalist?

    _____

8. Name 2 citrus fruits:

    _____   _____

9. In music:

    a) which notes fall on the lines? _____

    b) which notes fall in the spaces between lines? _____

    c) what does this sign ⨍ tell you to do? _____

Play and Poetry Readings

Multiple copies of plays from old school magazines or other sources are kept on file in some rooms. The rule of thumb seems to be 'as many copies as there are characters in the play'. Children often want to return to these again and again for an activity. As one teacher informed me, 'often a noisy group is banished to available space outside the room to engage in this activity'. Collections of poems can be similarly used. Many children enjoy **collaborative readings** of poems.

These represent just a small subset of the many activities which teachers can generate if they keep in mind the principles previously described. With a little thought and imagination they can be varied to suit any grade level or ability group.

F. Talking/interacting with learners

In these classrooms, teachers do a lot of talking **with** rather than talking **at** learners. Most of this 'talking with' takes place during activity time. This is the part of the language session when the teacher takes the opportunity to engage as many learners as possible in individual and/or small group interaction. During whole class focus time and SSR time, there is not the same opportunity to engage with the learners in an intensely interactive way. For example, in whole class focus time the teacher typically demonstrates through reading aloud or thinking aloud. Occasionally, the opportunity occurs to pose a question or make a response which results in some interaction. Essentially, however, it is activity time when the teacher gets the opportunity to use her own oral language in ways which will help learners develop many of the skills, awarenesses, knowledge and attitudes which they need in order to become effective, confident readers and writers.

The verbal interactions which teachers engage in with the students during this section of the language session can serve to facilitate such learning outcomes as:

★ bringing to conscious awareness (making explicit) many of the subtle relationships between knowledge of text forms, text conventions, text structure, the relationships between structure and function and the processes which can be used to produce texts effectively;

★ providing feedback about the degree of control which the learner has attained in any aspect(s) of reading, writing or learning;

★ coercing the learner into a 'justificatory' mode of thinking (the learner habitually offers a justification for, or evidential support for, any decisions he takes or opinions he canvasses);

★ supporting the notion of learner responsibility by coercing the learner to not only make choices from the options available to him but also to justify his choices and ultimately learn to live with them;

★ communicating expectations about individuals and their levels of achievement and application;

★ providing a model of problem identification/solving strategies by modelling the kinds of questions learners can ultimately ask of themselves;

★ learning about each individual student's needs, attitudes, strengths and weaknesses;

★ responding in ways which increase the probability that positive self-concepts and positive attitudes towards literacy will develop.

During this activity time, if the right kinds of activities have been designed and/or selected by the teacher, we have the situation of the learner deeply engaged with an enterprise which involves him in reading, writing, talking and listening ('language-ing') for real (as opposed to contrived) purposes, interacting with a 'more expert other' for the express purpose of getting some kind of response which will support his language learning. The 'co-occurrence' of all these factors must surely increase the probability of engagement with whatever demonstrations or feedback that are provided. In some ways it represents the optimal teaching/learning 'moment'. For these reasons, activity time is a crucial period of the language session. That's why I recommend that it get at least half the allocated session time.

What should teachers actually do during activity time?

I stated earlier that this period of the language session is an extremely busy period. It's so busy that attempts to capture what happens and subsequently analyse it present some complex problems to researchers. What follows, attempts to distil what I've recorded and observed after countless hours in classrooms where teachers were, in my opinion, successfully implementing a whole language/natural learning philosophy.

Teachers are constantly roving.

During this period, teachers continually move from child to child or group to group. Some do it quite systematically; others appear to move without any apparent, predetermined plan. Systematic or not, movement around the sites where children are engaging with their learning is essential.

Teacher/learner interactions are relatively short.

The majority of interactions which occur are less than one minute. Very rarely do they go beyond two minutes but they can. There is no hard and fast rule. If a teacher decides that a learner or group of learners needs more time, then she should give it to them.

The 'shape' of the interaction

While there is no one definitive method of engaging in these interactions, there are some basic 'moves' which teachers I've observed frequently employ:

a) **Seeking clarification of the learner's intent.**
   This is usually the first move after contact is made. It could be called a typical opening gambit. There are lots of ways to get the learner to clarify his intent. The simplest is to ask a question such as:
   "What are you doing?"
   "What are you trying to do?"
   "What are you supposed to be doing?"

   There are, of course, many possible variations of these questions. As long as the aim is achieved of making the learner verbalise what his task is or what strategies/processes he might use or what he thinks his problem might be, then the opening gambit has been successful.

b) **Listening to the learner's response.**
   After the opening move (clarification of intent), the teacher usually listens to the learner's response. Mostly, teachers just nod in an interested way or they say "uh-huh" as they nod. Whatever they do, the message which is communicated to the learner is, 'I find your response worthwhile and I'm listening to it.'

c) **Accepting the learner's response.**
   Again there are numerous ways of signalling that the response has been accepted for what it is — the learner's genuine attempt to state his intentions.

d) **Moves which follow acceptance.**
   After accepting the learner's response, there is a range of possible verbal moves which the teacher can make. Whichever move is

made it is a function of many interacting factors, including what she knows about the learner's strengths/weaknesses and previous learning; her expectations of the learner as a learner; and the quality of whatever work or product with which the learner has engaged.

Here are the most commonly occurring moves I've noticed in my research:

Focusing — Focusing on a gap in learner knowledge/skill, the teacher responds to the learner's attempt with a quick demonstration there and then of a perceived need.

Extending — "What else will you (could you, should you) do?" Extending is usually the move which occurs if the teacher is satisfied with the child's attempt to clarify and state his intent and decides to raise the ante.

Refocusing — "Is this what you're trying to say (do, write), or is it something else?" Teachers usually refocus if the statement of intent is confused, ambiguous and obviously unclear in the learner's mind, or if the draft or task being worked on is obviously not on course.

Redirecting — Teachers redirect when they make a judgement that the learner's product or draft of a task being done either does not match the stated intent, or does not match the expectations which the teacher holds of the learner. Teachers usually redirect by making a quick decision about what they think the learner needs to control in order to complete that task. Then, they either provide a demonstration or send the learner off to another source of expertise. For example:

"I think you should just work on getting the ideas organised in the right order now, and come back to the problem of those words which you think you've misspelled, later. Go and ask Melissa to listen to what you've done so far and see if she can help you get those ideas in the right sequence."

Is that all there is to it?

Of course not. Any attempt to reconstruct the busy ebb and flow of classroom behaviour will inevitably simplify what really happens. There is a lot more taking place during these interactions than I've managed to capture and synthesise. For example, every one of the moves I've described requires a response from the learner to which the teacher must again respond. One pattern of response which has emerged from some of my data is this:

Learners' responses to teachers' extending or refocusing moves are usually accompanied by an explicit request for justification or further clarification.

For example:

Teacher: (extending) "What else could you do?"
Learner: "I could change the next section so that it tells about the characters in the book."
Teacher: "Why do you want to do that?"

The teacher's final question is an example of a request for justification. While the possible variations of this kind of request are many, I've noticed that teachers seem to develop a personal repertoire of ways of making these request, for example:

> "What do you mean by that?"
> "Go on, convince me that that's a good idea for your piece (task, etc.)."
> "How do you know that? Find me some examples in the text to support that."

These requests for justification/clarification are continually being made and thread their way through and around most of the verbal interactions which occur between teacher and learners during this intensely busy period. Soon they become second nature. Learners internalise the teacher's constant demand for justification/clarification and ultimately ask the question of themselves. Teachers know this internalisation has taken place when the learners automatically offer the justification.

Other verbal behaviours

Making connections: The kinds of moves and requests which I've described are supported by other kinds of verbal behaviours. One common verbal strategy which teachers employ is what I've called 'making connections'.

Teachers make connections at any time during the language session — when they're in whole class focus time, during SSR, during activity time or during sharing time. Typically, they just break into whatever is happening, make the connection, and then return to what it was they were doing. It's a kind of hit-and-run, pedagogical move, almost incidental to the ongoing classroom business. The implicit message is: *Here's another piece of information about texts and text-making that you might be able to make use of in your reading and writing tasks. Tune in if it's relevant or store it away for future use. I'm not going to dwell on it or make a big deal about it.*

The connections teachers bring to the learners' conscious awarenesses are typically connections between texts or connections between the processes which are used to make texts. They make these connections by making explicit the kinds of links that exist between such aspects of texts as:

a) **characters** ("When I read 'Boy', which is Road Dahl's autobiography, I recognised some of the characters from his books. Listen." She reads two descriptive passages about characters from two different books.)

b) **text forms** ("Chelsea has just completed a fable which she wrote herself. It's only short so I'll read it to you. See if you think it really is a fable. Or is it more like a story?" Of course, any response is accompanied by a request for clarification/justification.)

These connections can also be made between plots, authors, illustrators, events, leads, different text organisation and a host of other text characteristics.

Teachers make connections between processes by sharing with learners such things as how one learns to spell (by reading and writing) and how a lead sentence from a book can be changed and used in personal writing. For example:

Context: Activity time. Pupils are engaged in various activities. The teacher has just interacted with Cindy about a piece of writing she is working on. The teacher suddenly looks up and talks to the whole class.

> **Teacher:** "Just stop what you're doing for a moment and listen to Cindy's lead sentence. I think it's very good."
>
> **Cindy:** (Reading from her draft) "I remember it as if it were yesterday . . ."
>
> **Teacher:** "Where did you get the idea for that? It's a lead that really wants to make me keep on reading."
>
> **Cindy:** "I read it in 'Treasure Island' and changed it a bit to suit my piece. Right at the very beginning, 'I remember him as if it were esterday, as he came to the inn door. A huge, hairy, nut-brown man, his tarry pigtail falling over the shoulder of his soiled blue coat.' " (Sic.)
>
> **Teacher:** "Yes, often you get good ideas for your own writing from the books you read, don't you?"

The teacher then signals that the hit-and-run is over. She moves on to the next interaction.

I want to emphasise that what I have described here as verbal behaviours are a distillation of principles derived from many hours of observation of teachers and interacting with learners. I am not suggesting that these are the only verbal behaviours that teachers can or should bring to bear in the classroom. Nor am I suggesting that all teachers need to do is rote memorise the few simple patterns of moves that I've described and apply them verbatim to each child or group of children. How teachers interact with learners, what they actually say and how often they say it, is a consequence of many things. I've tried on numerous occasions to find out what those teachers, who seem to be most proficient at verbally interacting with learners, carry around inside their heads as they engage in these interactions. What emerges from the many interviews I've had with them is that what they actually decide to say when they're interacting with learners is determined by a variety of factors, including:

— their understanding of how learning works (their language plan),
— their understanding of the relationships between the different forms of language,
— their aims with respect to literacy learning in their class,
— their expectations of the child with whom they're interacting — this, of course, presupposes a great deal of knowledge about each child's strengths,
— how well they listen to what each child tells them during the interactions which they have.

I have tried to sum up in figure 8 the nature of the verbal interactions which I've been trying to describe in words.

G. Monitoring and evaluating literacy development

How does one keep track of and evaluate the kinds of learning/ achievement (or lack of it) in a classroom that operates along whole language/natural learning principles? Traditional approaches to monitoring and evaluating through standardised tests or check lists in reading, writing and spelling simply cannot be applied to these classrooms.

This is because traditional procedures are based on assumptions that are quite different from those which underpin the holistic/natural view of learning. Reading ages and numerical grades, for example, assume that the various forms of language behaviour (reading, spelling, writing, talking, phonic ability, etc.) are separate, independent domains of knowledge and/or expertise and that a score on some kind of test/checklist represents some kind of static, immutable degree of learning, knowledge or skill that the learner has reached therein. Kemp explains why these assumptions cannot be applied to a holistic approach to learning language, thus:

' ... in a developmental context of wholistic approaches to literacy, an inspection of a child's error transcript of oral reading, or of his or her successive versions of a valued, original self-edited story, and of changes that have evolved in spelling accuracy through story writing, all show that these (language) functions shift not only from occasion to occasion, but also within the occasion. Development in literacy is not linear. Nor is it by definition static. Accepting these assumptions of assessment in a wholistic literacy curriculum makes that assessment much more difficult than it used to be because it is change that is being measured, not stability, and this requires that the teacher must be eternally vigilant.'
(Kemp, 1986, p. 219)

The Pattern of Teacher/Pupil Interactions during Activity Time

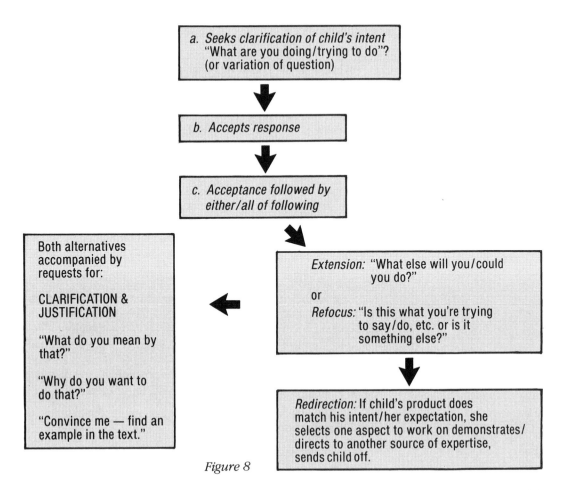

Figure 8

How does one maintain such eternal vigilance? The simple answer is that one continually builds up a store of knowledge about each child's literacy development.

In this sense, the teacher becomes like a classical anthropologist. Like an anthropologist, she alternates between participant observer, detached observer and collector of artifacts. At times she observes the 'members of the tribe' from a distance, recording her observations for later analysis. At other times she asks questions of various informants about what they know and think and about the ways they produce their artifacts, all the time recording their responses. Her records become her store of knowledge. From this store of knowledge she tries to construct what reality is for the tribe or culture she's observing. In the case of the teacher building a store of knowledge about literacy development, the reality she is trying to construct is how each one of her pupils' knowledge and skill in literacy and all that it entails is changing and developing over time.

This process of building a store of knowledge begs two very complex prior questions.

1) What kinds of knowledge does one build up a store of?

The answer to this question is related to the aims and objectives which one has set. This is why there is no definitive, conclusive set of standards or levels which can be applied universally to each grade level or age group. In other words, just as each teacher will have to develop her own set of aims and objectives, so she will have to make decisions about what kinds of information she needs to collect in order to assess and evaluate her pupils' literacy learning. Just as each teacher's aims and objectives will be contingent upon what they know and value about literacy and its various manifestations (reading, writing, spelling, speaking, and so on), so the kinds of knowledge that they need to continuously build up about the learners in their class will be contingent upon the same things. Therefore I cannot give the definitive set of assessment and evaluative criteria which teachers can immediately apply to their own classrooms. I can, however, do what I did with respect to the development of aims and objectives, and describe the kinds of knowledge that I would build up and why I would do it. The kinds of criteria I would use for assessment or evaluation are idiosyncratic to me, based on my values and what I know and understand about literacy.

How Cambourne would do it:

I would wish to build up a store of knowledge from two different kinds of data.

(i) data which permitted me to draw conclusions about each learner's attitudes towards literacy and literacy learning; (**Rationale**: If I want those whom I'm teaching to continue to use reading and writing after they've left my classroom they must feel positive about themselves as readers and writers and positive towards the continued use of reading, writing and other forms of language.)

(ii) data which permitted me to draw conclusions about each learner's developing control of the processes which underpin effective language use, especially the processes which underpin effective text construction using reading, writing and oral forms of language. (**Rationale**: Effective language use, in all its manifestations, is contingent upon both knowing **about**, and doing things **with**, language. In order to read or write effectively one must operate **on** text a certain way. One must bring into play certain processes.)

Where do such data come from?

Teachers collect them in two main ways: a) by systematically observing learners in language-using situations and recording what they observe, and b) by systematically collecting artifacts which the learners produce in the language sessions and analysing them.

2) How does one organise oneself to collect such data?

Here are some generalisations about organising oneself for monitoring and evaluating development which I'm able to make from my research data. They represent a synthesis of what I've observed teachers actually do and from what they've told me in interview situations about what they do. These generalisations take the form of decisions which teachers need to make:

(i) Deciding on a method of recording observations

Most teachers I've observed/questioned about this aspect of organising oneself get themselves a hardcovered exercise book and divide it into sections that correspond to each child in the class. Each child typically is allotted between three — five blank pages. This book is given various titles by the teachers who use them, e.g. Anecdotal Records, Observations, Notes on Children's Achievements. The hard cover is essential because this book is carried constantly by the teacher during the language sessions. It gets opened and closed many times and in the busy ebb and flow of classroom life it can come in for some rough treatment. In short, it must be sturdy.

(ii) Deciding on a routine for recording observations

There are two kinds of decision that need to be made with respect to deciding on a routine for recording observations:

a) when to record them
b) what to record

'When to record' is a relatively easy decision to make. Observations can be made and data collected during each of the segments of the language session, i.e., during whole class focus, SSR, activity and sharing time.

The 'what to record' decision is not as easy because it presupposes a set of criteria of language development which can be inferred from certain observable behaviours (markers) which learners display while being observed. Such markers are based on what the teacher knows, values and understands about learning, language, language development, reading, writing, speaking, etc. These markers should also be related to the literacy curriculum or agenda which the teacher is trying to implement.

While I cannot give a sure-fire, universal set of markers, I can describe a set which teachers who have been co-researchers with me in developing the theory which permeates this book have developed and implemented. In order to do this I need to introduce in more detail the concept of markers and how they might be used.

(iii) The concept of markers

What are markers?
Overt forms of language behaviour which mark or give evidence of the presence of some kind of linguistic knowledge, or skill, or attitude.

Where do markers come from?
The values and knowledge teachers and the community hold about language and language use.

For what purpose do teachers use them?
To inform their judgements about children's language development.

Which markers should teachers use?
There is no one set of universal markers which are used, without variation, every time language behaviour is observed.

The markers which teachers use will vary:

a) according to purpose and audience of the language situation being observed,
b) according to what teachers value and/or think is 'good' language use,
c) as teachers learn more about language and language use.

Some General Characteristics of Language Control

Despite the relative nature of values, knowledge and understandings, there are some kinds of linguistic knowledge, skills and attitudes which teachers generally agree are important and therefore worthy of development. These include:

1. Sense of audience when communicating.
2. Control of conventions appropriate to language context.
3. Ability to use of a range of registers/genres.
4. Vocabulary acquisition and use appropriate to context.
5. Control of grammatical options.
6. Confidence in using language in different contexts.

The above are all productive language skills. Certain receptive language skills are equally as important and worthy of development:

7. Comprehension of what's been heard or read.
8. Listening attentively.

How does one recognise that these agreed-upon characteristics of 'good' or 'desirable' language use are present or absent in learners' repertoires? In the section which follows, markers of these characteristics which teachers have found useful are described.

Markers of Characteristics of Control of Language

★ **Consistent** occurrence of markers is evidence of a **high degree** of control.

★ **Inconsistent** use of markers or approximations is evidence of **growing** control.

★ **Absence** of markers is evidence of **lack** of control.

1. Sense of audience when communicating is marked by:

a) Recognition of audience's degree of background information.
b) Recognition of presence or lack of shared knowledge/values in audience through choice of words or form of language.
c) Use of pronouns, e.g., explanations of who 'he', 'she', etc. is in retelling or sharing an experience.

2. Control of conventions appropriate to language contexts

a) Control of the conventions of published written language is
marked by:

- accurate spelling
- correct punctuation
- legible handwriting
- correct use of standard English grammar (c.f. 6 below)

b) Control of the conventions of 'published' spoken language is
marked by:

- correct pronunciation
- correct use of standard English grammar
- appropriate intonation and expression

3. Ability to use a range of registers is marked by:

a) Textual form appropriate to purpose and audience.

b) Vocabulary appropriate to audience and purpose,
e.g., colloquialisms.

c) Recognition of common characteristics of the form of text used,
e.g., report, narrative, instruction, recount, exposition.

d) Inclusion of common characteristics of the form of text used.

e) Setting out appropriate to form of text.

f) Recognition of stylistic devices and techniques used by other
authors. (Authorcraft)

g) Use of stylistic devices and techniques used by other authors.

h) Inclusion of metaphor, analogy and simile appropriate to context.

**4. Vocabulary acquisition and use appropriate to context are
marked by:**

a) Vocabulary appropriate to register.

b) Use of a range of synonyms.

c) Use of unusual or new words in writing and speaking.

d) Willingness to seek meanings of unknown words.

e) Use of precise terms, e.g., 'warm' instead of 'a bit hot'.

f) Specialist vocabulary, e.g., 'body' of water rather than 'block' when
map-reading.

g) Use of vocabulary to create special effects.

h) Spillover of vocabulary from one context to another, e.g., the use
in writing or speech of words and phrases from material which
has been previously read or heard, and vice versa.

5. Control of grammatical options is marked by:

a) Appropriate use of tenses.

b) Appropriate use of pronouns.

c) Appropriate use of prepositions.

d) Absence of over-generalisational *(e.g. runned, mouses)*.

e) Ability to paraphrase (indicates a high degree of control of syntax
and vocabulary).

f) Logical sentence construction.

g) Sentence complexity. (Young children use short, simple sentences, often joined by 'and' and 'then'. Mature language users may also make appropriate use of longer, more complex sentences by combining sentences and ideas. For example 'The dog chased the cat *which* lived next door' is a more complex sentence than either of the two sentences which formed it: 'The dog chased the cat. The cat lived next door.')

h) The range and number of conjunctions used. (Conjunctions signal logical relationships between what comes before them and what comes after them. The range and type of conjunctions which are used regularly, signal the kinds of logical connections that language users can articulate. Immature language users use a limited number of conjunctions and often use them inappropriately.)

Types of conjunctions:
i   **Temporal:** while, before, as, since, when . . .
ii   **Causal:** because, since, as, for . . .
iii   **Concessional:** though, although . . .
iv   **Conditional:** for, if, unless, whether . . .
v   **Purpose:** for, so . . .
vi   **Comparative:** as, than, like . . .
vii   **Inferential:** Therefore, as . . .
viii **Adversative:** but, however, nevertheless . . .
ix   **Additive:** and, moreover, furthermore . . .
x   **Disjunctive:** or, nor, least, otherwise . . .
xi   **Additive/disjunctive:** and/or, either/or . . .

Note that the same conjunction can indicate different logical relationships depending on the context:
Since you went away, we've bought a new car. (**Temporal link**)
Since you broke the window, you'll have to pay for it.(**Causal link**)

Note, too, that the same word (e.g. like) can serve different grammatical functions:
He took off like a rocket. (**Comparative conjunction**)
I like chocolate more than is good for me. (**Verb, not a conjunction**)

6. Confidence in using language in different language contexts is marked by willingness to:

a) Share information during sharing sessions.

b) Volunteer comments and/or answer questions during sharing sessions.

c) Question others during sharing sessions.

d) Respond to questions and criticisms about what was said during sharing.

127

e) Use language for a variety of purposes and audiences.

f) Attempt new language tasks.

7. Comprehension of what's been heard or read is marked by:

a) Understanding shown in answers to questions or associated activities.

b) How well the child's sharing of texts which have been read or written reflects the original text in main ideas, balance of detail, theme, sequence, etc.

c) Coherence of any retellings or sharings which are done.

d) Evidence of specific levels of comprehension, e.g.:

Low Level — lists of unrelated items, no evidence of selection.

Moderate Level — some degree of coherence, some evidence of selection.

High Level — ability to coherently select main points and generalise to other examples.

8. Listening attentively is marked by:

a) Comprehension of what's been heard (see above).

b) Asking clarifying questions when necessary.

c) Appropriate response to instructions.

d) Often, overt listening behaviours (e.g. concentration).

It is important to realise that this set of markers represents a *synthesis* of many different lists of markers trialled by a number of teachers. Not one teacher of those who worked on the theory which underpins this book used all of them. It would be an impossible task for any teacher to attempt to identify and use all of these markers in any one language session,

What most teachers do is to use only a few of them at any one time. Those which are used are a function of the context and purpose of the language activity which is being observed.

Thus, during a sharing session in which one child is retelling a book which has been read during SSR, the teacher's focus may be on **some** of those markers which are associated with confidence, comprehension and the logical order of materials. During activity time, the focus may be on **some** markers which inform the teacher of the sense of audience or the control of register, or of grammatical complexity.

The following case study is an example of how one teacher used some of these markers and how she recorded her observations in her Observation Book.

CASE STUDY — Adrian (Year 5)

15/2: Observed during retelling activity. A's predictions were good, his actual retelling well-sequenced, sensitive, some good vocab., no punct!!!

22/2: Observed while working on activity involving information for 'Stone-Age Man' task. Skim-read for information. First time I knew he knew how to do it.

25/2: Had brief reading conference with A. Reading *First Fleet*. Non-fiction. Says he enjoyed the illustrations, says he chose it for the humour.

14/3: Conferenced about poem he's working on (Uncle Jake). Very slow to get going this year. Knows how to correct metre but hasn't done this fully. Must keep helping re attitude/output.

26/3: Observed during SSR. Was deeply engaged with *Barney Boofe and the Cricket Bat.*

2/4: Observed during SSR. A is fully engaged when reading and is covering fiction/non-fiction/poetry. His comprehension so far has been very sound.

11/4: Conferenced during activity time. A working on a piece of writing. Was a great idea that went nowhere. He decided I was right and is fixing it up — meaning unclear.

12/4: Today A shared a fiction book he'd read. Comprehension was very sound.

18/4: Talked with him during activity time about letter he was working on. Was a very well-structured letter, with a good account of some of his experiences at camp.

29/4: Has finished a story **White Wolf**. Excellent story in two chapters. Included glossary!! to explain pronouns 'him', 'his', 'he'. Probably because at sharing time Melissa complained that when he read it out she got mixed up about who 'him' etc. really were. Says he picked up glossary idea from some non-fiction he's been reading. Admits he was being facetious and 'having a friendly go at Melissa'. Explained he would ordinarily rework the pronouns so they were clear.

Term 2

16/5: A is very much into non-fiction. Says he finds this material new and therefore more interesting and absorbing than fiction.

27/5: Reading like a writer!!! Realised his crocodile piece 'lacked information and was too general'. At sharing time he shared an article he read about pharaohs. Commented it was 'poor writing' because 'it lacked information and was too general'.

19/6: Some reflections on A's participation in sharing sessions this term: As a questioner, asks peers some very penetrating questions and picks them up re flaws in logic. Must be listening closely. As a sharer provides a structured and thorough summary of what he's read as in *BFG* (Big Friendly Giant) and *Poisonous Reptiles.*

15/7: Participation in story grammar activity with his group showed him to have a very perceptive idea of the relationships in 'Storm Boy'. Obviously has comprehended the story.

3/8: Poetry for contract?? see 14/3, ditto! Has spent a lot of time reading the models in *Mad* magazine, has tried a few drafts but doesn't appear to be interested in working them through to publication. Should I encourage??

20/8: Sharing. A shared some lovely pieces of poetry he'd written. Said he'd been saving them up for about six weeks. So much for my observation of 3/8!!

Using Learners to Assist in Data Collection

Teachers can ease the burden of data collection if they set up procedures whereby the learners themselves keep records of their language achievements throughout the year. A reading log which records what has been read, when it was commenced and finished, and how it ranked on a scale of Like/Dislike, is a way of keeping track of what different students are reading. It can also form the basis for short reading conferences during which much can be discovered about the degrees of comprehension, the depth of understanding, the use of different reading strategies, and so on.

NAME *NEILL. P*

TITLE & AUTHOR	VALUE LINE 1 2 3 4 5					TYPE OF BOOK	ACTIVITY
Mulga Bills Bicyle	*	*	*	⊙	*	4fP	
Revolting Rhymes roald Dahls	*	*	*	*	⊙	HfP	~~———~~
The man from snowing River By AB Patesern	*	*	*	*	⊛	P	F.6
Henry And Bee zus	*	*	*	✳	*	F H	
a Bush chirsting AB Paterson	*	*	⊙	*	*	fP	
Book for Kids SJ. Dennis	*	*	*	✗	*	fP	
Captain Beacky and his oband.	*	*	*	✗		NfP	
Quick silver Book 3	*	*	*	✳	*	Fontasyne	
~~As~~ Inside childerns information	*	*	*	*	∞✳	NF	
Ausfarlian endanged wild life Frank Manobn	✳	*	*	*	*	NF	
Follow that Bus Pax Huthins	*	*	*	*	*	F H	F.1
Explore N3	*	*	✳	*	*		
Here comes chailie moon Shirley Huges	*	*	*	✳	ooooo✳	F H	1.6
Romona and her Father Beavrly cleary	*	*	*	✳	*	FH	
Cricket Magazine	*	*	*	✳		NEFH	
Jumanji	✳	*	*	*	*	FH	
Thalia The Failara	*	*	✳	*	*	F. H	

One teacher I've worked with encourages her learners to keep reflective journals. Every day, immediately after morning recess, everyone writes for ten minutes in their learning journals. They reflect on what they learned in language each day, what puzzled them, and how they solved problems. Over time these become fascinating records of the growth of reflective thinking, of meta-textual awareness and a variety of other language-related abilities.

> Sherrie 15/7/88
>
> You have to have time to think insed rushing into it

Sherrie has realised something about her own learning processes.

> 22/7/88
>
> Charts help me with my spelling because I always look there and read it then it clikes in my head for along time

Sherrie is 'scrounging'. She is taking responsibility for her own learning.

> 31/7/88
>
> Also I recen I learn by me woking out thing insted of mrs brown giving as the ansaw because I don't learn like that

More evidence of taking responsibility.

(iv) Deciding on which artifacts to collect

As well as observing, recording and interpreting learners' ongoing behaviour, another source of valuable data about change is to be found in the artifacts which learners produce. Usually these artifacts are the result of the activities which learners are expected to complete. Typically they are written but if the activities have been chosen wisely, they represent the end result of a great deal of reading, talking, listening, drafting, thinking and 'language-ing'.

As the focus for evaluation in a holistic/natural classroom is 'change over time', teachers need to decide how often they wish to collect artifacts for the purpose of evaluating. Again there is nothing definitive. If I were to describe how the mythical, 'average', whole-language teacher operated, she would do something like this:

She would select between three and five pieces of writing from across a range of genres — one narrative, a couple of expository (say a report and an instructional piece) and a poem — per term. This is a rate of about one piece every three to five weeks. These pieces would have been worked on up to pre-publication stage. They would represent the best that the learner can do without help from the teacher or from other pupils. These pieces would be photocopied and stapled to a blank sheet of paper. The teacher would then write comments pertaining to whatever the piece informed her of the learner's control of language, for examples, control over the conventions of spelling, punctuation and grammar, or information, vocabulary, organisation of materials and sequencing. If a specific genre form, e.g. a report, it may inform her of the control over that form. These would then be fixed in the hardcovered, observation book on the appropriate page, near the observations which the teacher has been making on that specific child.

Here is an example from a Grade 5 teacher:

Obviously the degree to which the pieces inform the teacher of the learner's development over time will be a function of what the teacher knows about such things as text structure (the markers which identify different genre), language development, the processes of reading and writing, the conventions of spelling, punctuation, grammar, learning and literacy, and what she values and considers to be important.

No book can give a universal recipe for these things for all teachers. The generalisation I can draw from my data, over time, is that the more teachers know and understand of language, learning and literacy, the more each piece they examine will inform them.

Educated teachers are in a better position to evaluate and monitor literacy learning.

There are other avenues for collecting developmental data. One teacher I know has developed a technique for using learners' written retellings of texts. She selects (or sometimes writes herself) a piece of narrative or expository text and presents it to the children in a specially devised lesson procedure. The outcome of the procedure *(see Brown & Cambourne, 1987)* is a written retelling of the text, done under very natural, non-stressful conditions. These retellings reflect how well the learner has read, comprehended and re-translated that text form. They inform the teacher of many aspects of the control that the learner has over a number of language forms (reading, writing) and of many conventions, as well as vocabulary, genre, ability to paraphrase and so on.

Other teachers are trialling editing and proofreading procedures. These vary from teacher to teacher. Generally, these procedures involve asking a child's permission to photocopy a draft of something he's written and asking others to work on it as an editor would. The editorial changes they suggest, and the proofreading they do, reveal a great deal about the knowledge they carry around inside their heads about literacy, language, the conventions of spelling, etc. One or two of these per term can add to the store of information being built up.

Some teachers who are familiar with the many variations of miscue analysis and/or error analysis procedures also like to sample learners' oral reading at certain times of the school year and add these to the store of knowledge as well.

(v) Deciding on how to synthesise the store of knowledge

Once the teacher has compiled a store of information about the literacy development of each child in her class, she has to make some kind of coherent sense of it. Again, in this respect she is not unlike the classical field anthropologist who makes sense out of her observations and reflections by reading them again and again. Themes, categories and patterns usually emerge as she 'massages' the data. When they do, they become the 'organisers' around which interpretation and explanation of the culture she is observing are structured. One could argue that they are the organisers of the reality she constructs which is a function of her own familiarity with the culture, the data collection procedures she uses, and all of her background experiences, values and so on.

Teachers have to do much the same thing with the data they collect. Unfortunately, they don't have the same amount of time nor the same kind of freedom to interpret as does the field anthropologist. They need to devise how to categorise their data in ways that inform them and, if necessary, will enable them to inform others of the development of learners for whom they are responsible. The categories they devise will, of course, be strongly tied to their aims and objectives which are in turn closely related to what they know and believe about literacy development. Again, no one can supply these categories for them. They must work them through themselves.

Although it sounds a little daunting, those teachers whom I've been observing and questioning generally agree that it takes a few hours at the most. The categories which are developed do change from year to year as they learn more, but once done, these teachers can never go back to using anyone else's.

Typically, the categories they do devise take the form of checklist statements. The checklists on pages 86 and 87 are an example of what I mean. She began with two Language Evaluation Sheets — one for reading, one for writing. As a consequence of reading through the data she collected, she felt confident about making definitive statements about each child's development in the various categories she devised. Each child's summary sheet (really a checklist) was attached to his section of the Observation Book.

(See pages 86-87.)

I know there will be teachers who will look at this sample checklist and think: *"I'll use that one. Why should I bother to work out my own?"*

Forget it. It won't work for you. In the whole language classroom you must be like your learners. You must take responsibility for your own monitoring and evaluation. You can't borrow anyone else's unless you are a clone of that person, with the same aims, background knowledge, values and experiences. The only checklists that ever work are those which are grounded in one's own observations and belief systems.

7

Theory into Practice III

This is the third chapter which deals with the concept of theory into practice. It is different from the two which precede it. Chapter 5 is an expansion and elaboration of the theory which is detailed in Chapter 4. Chapter 6 is a description of the actions teachers can take and the things they can do in order to get the theory working at the classroom level. This chapter is written in response to a question which I've been frequently asked by teachers who express an interest in the whole language/natural learning theory of literacy education. The question is usually a variation of this:

Okay, I know the theory and understand it; you've given me some ideas for getting the theory working in the classroom, but what does a classroom which puts all of these principles into practice actually look like?

The final stage of the theory-into-practice journey attempts to actually visualise the theory which, up to this point, has been described out of context. Accordingly, what follows is an attempt to capture, at the descriptive level, what a typical whole language classroom looks like. It reads a little like a film script because it is, in fact, a verbal paraphrase of what is captured on the research video tapes which I've made in the course of trying to discover what makes such classrooms tick. I will break into the script at frequent intervals to identify, describe and explain how the theory and the practice are coming together in the scenes which we're going to observe.

ACT ONE Scene One

The Setting

It is 9.10 a.m. on a typical morning at Balarang Primary School. The Grade 5 classroom is vacant while the 32 children and their teacher, Mrs Brown, are assembling outside in the playground with the rest of the school. The bell which signals the end of play has just sounded and teachers and children are moving toward the assembly section of the playground. Once assembled they will be welcomed to school by the teacher on duty and any housekeeping matters concerning the smooth running of the day will be relayed to them before they move off towards their separate classrooms.

The Grade 5 classroom which the children will enter at the conclusion of the short assembly is of standard size. There is a chalkboard on one wall (probably intended to be the front of the classroom by the government architect who designed the building) and a bench, with a sink and taps, runs all the way along the opposite wall (obviously intended to be the back of the room). There are numerous standard bookshelves and storage cupboards (obviously government supply) placed against other walls. The number of moveable, table-type desks and chairs in the room is slightly greater than the number of children on the class roll. In terms of size and of the furniture which is in it, the room is typical of many other classrooms around the country.

In other respects, however, it is unique. The walls are filled with charts which contain a great deal of writing. These charts appear to be a mixture of those created by the teacher and those which have been created by the children. The children's charts appear to be summaries of the works of children's authors. There are charts about Roald Dahl, Beverly Cleary, Robin Klein, May Gibbs, Banjo Patterson, Henry Lawson, Enid Blyton, Colin Thiele — to name just a few. A careful reading of the charts reveals them to be what could be called primitive reports. Among other things, they consist of lists of the books which each author has written, accounts of some of the events, characters, plots and similarities and differences within and between these books, freely sprinkled with quotes and illustrative examples. As well as author reports, there are charts from individual children which are reports of a recent expedition the class undertook to the nearby lake in order to observe the behaviour of the herring gull.

The charts made by the teacher appear to be of two kinds: Those concerned mainly with information to help the children of the class with their reading and writing tasks (reference charts) and those which appear to be summaries of discussions which have occurred (summary charts). An example of the first kind is one about the value and importance of leads in writing; another is the one which lists synonyms for words such as 'nice' and 'cried out' and 'run'. On the opposite wall is another of this type; it lists the specific details of the class 'contract' for Term 1.

As well as the reference charts, there are several summary charts. One of these indicates that the class has recently finished a study of fables and fairy tales. The chart is a reflection of the discussion that obviously occurred as a consequence of the immersion in these two related genres. Another is the summary of the criteria which make up a report.

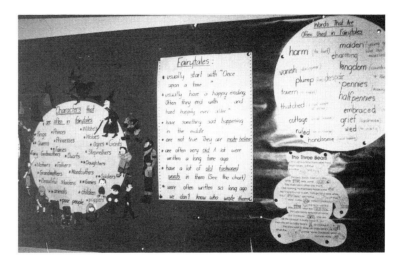

The way in which the desks in this classroom are set out is also atypical. They are not arranged in serried rows facing the front. Rather, they are organised in two columns so that children, when seated, face each other and are side on to the architect-designed front of the room. Mrs Brown's floor plan is shown on page 99.

Notes on the script (a) The Setting

The setting is one which has been moulded by the activities which take place there, i.e. the physical arrangements of the furniture, space and artifacts all fit in with the purpose and functions which the setting serves.

The arrangement of the desks increases the probability that the problems, issues and concerns which learners will be faced with while 'language-ing', will be addressed by groups rather than individuals. Learners will find it very difficult **not** to interact with each other, sharing the problems which they encounter and the solutions or partial solutions to them. Group discussions of how things can be done with language are demonstrations of how others use and apply language to meet certain needs. Such demonstrations are also a means of making explicit much of the implicit knowledge about language and language use that learners must have.

The charts in the room obviously reflect the commitment to visual immersion in language forms. They are also demonstrations of how language which is used to report and inform is structured. Furthermore, they become references from which learners can scrounge details of forms, structures, spellings, etc. which they might need in order to complete similar tasks. They also provide the raison d'etre for engaging in all of the language behaviours which were employed in their production, viz., one needs to read and understand a range of Roald Dahl's books if one is going to convince one's fellow students that it is a worthwhile enterprise to engage with his works. In order to inform and report, one also needs to engage with the demonstrations of these forms (genre) and with the processes that are used to produce them. One also needs to get some feedback and response to one's initial attempts (approximations) to create texts which do this.

Finally, the contract charts reflect the commitment to the notion of learner responsibility. These are constant reminders of the options from which learners have to choose each day. These choices represent the beginnings of taking responsibility for making decisions about what will be engaged with and what will be ignored. Thus, before the actors even enter the setting, the scene is one which is set in such a way that, given the right script, certain forms of behaviour will follow.

Lights, Camera, Action

At 9.15 a.m. the children enter the room and stand behind their chairs. Mrs Brown greets them with 'Good morning' and they respond in kind. She then moves to the left-hand side of the chalkboard and sits down with a book in her hand. The children, after removing their writing implements from their school bags, move to the open floor space in front of her chair and sit on the floor in a rough semicircle. Some of the bigger children bring their chairs and place them around the outside of this semicircle. Mrs Brown waits for the children to be settled comfortably then opens the book and says:

*"We've been reading **Tom's Midnight Garden** for the last couple of days and we've reached a very interesting stage of the story. Where did we get to yesterday?"*

About two-thirds of the children raise their hands. Mrs Brown selects Natasha, who is sitting in about the middle of the group. Natasha offers a retelling of the events which have occurred so far. Her retelling is more than a sequential account of the events and characters in the story. It is coherent and unified. She has obviously selected and organised what she considers to be the most salient features of the storyline, retelling it with consideration for her audience, rarely using pronouns to refer to characters unless she first resolves each pronoun's referent. In other words she rarely uses a 'he', 'she', 'him', 'them' or 'it' in an ambiguous way.

Mrs Brown signals that she accepts Natasha's retelling by listening attentively and thanking her. She then says:

> *"That's a good retelling, Natasha. You've captured very effectively the essence and the main points of the plot structure and character traits."*

She then makes a statement and follows it up with a question.

> *"This book is very unusual because of the way that Philippa Pearce treats time. How is the concept of time treated?"*

About one-third of the children raise their hands to respond. Mrs Brown selects Paul. His response triggers off more hand-raising and some calling out. Mrs Brown selects one more response and the class listens. By holding up the book Mrs Brown signals that she's going to continue reading. At 9.20 a.m. she begins reading. A deep hush settles over the group. She reads, uninterrupted for about seven minutes. She then stops and says:

> *"Listen to how the author creates atmosphere just here. I'm going to read that paragraph again."*

She reads it again and asks.

> *"What is she doing that helps create that eerie atmosphere, Chris?"*

Chris responds thus:

> *"She's using lots of dark words."*

Mrs Brown follows up Chris's response with a kind of probe.

> *"What do you mean — dark words?"*

Chris looks thoughtful for a minute and answers thus:

"Words that show feelings of fear, like 'gloomy' and 'cobwebs' and things like that."

Mrs Brown accepts Chris's rather global response and asks of the whole group:

"What other writer do we know who uses a similar technique to create atmosphere?"

About half the hands go up but before Mrs Brown can call on one child, Chelsea calls out:

"E B White, when he's describing the barn that Wilbur lives in and he gives all those details about smells and sounds and so on."

Mrs Brown says:

"That's right. It's a technique that a lot of writers use. Putting in detail like that keeps your reader interested. You might like to try it with your own writing."

She then continues reading. A deep hush again settles on the group. Mrs Brown reads for another seven minutes then closes the book. Some of the children use this opportunity to stretch their cramped legs or change the pressure on their bottoms. She then asks:

"When did Philippa Pearce write this book? It's different from her others that we've read. I wonder whether it was written earlier or later than the others?"

As if thinking aloud, and in answer to her own question, she keeps talking.

"Let me see . . . what is the book's publishing history? If I look on the imprint page just inside the cover I should find the date when the book was first published. Hmm, let me see. Oh, yes, here it is — it was published in London in 1958 which means she wrote it before the other one we've read. I wonder if she's one of those authors who write series that you should read in order if you wish to understand them properly? You know, like C S Lewis and the Narnia books."

This comment elicits a series of responses from the children about other books which Philippa Pearce has written and a discussion of which ones are related and not related. The discussion lasts for about five minutes and ranges over other books and authors who have and/or have not written a series.

Notes on the script (b) Scene 1

This opening scene is a smorgasbord of demonstrations with which learners can engage if they recognise the need to. These demonstrations are organised at a number of different levels. At the broadest, most macroscopic level, the book *Tom's Midnight Garden* is a demonstration of how the narrative form which we have labelled the 'novel' is structured in terms of such things as plot, characters, setting and use of a whole range of language systems. It reflects the commitment to aural immersion in language.

The invitation to volunteer a recount of the novel to the stage reached the previous day is a confirmation of the learning setting being a safe one. One volunteers only if one believes one is capable of meeting the demands of the situation. There is no pressure to perform. Natasha's recount is a demonstration of how one uses the oral form of the language to retell effectively in the context which has been set up. It is also a demonstration of how another person (a peer) has interpreted and selected information.

The teacher's second invitation to comment on the concept of time is a demonstration that speculation is not only condoned, it is expected. The blocks of time devoted to uninterrupted reading of the text provide demonstrations of how texts can be read and enjoyed. The interruptions to the text reading provide a multiplicity of demonstrations of how texts are written and how the information contained on the preliminary pages of a book may be used. Underlying these demonstrations are more subtle demonstrations of how information, skills, knowledge and texts are connected. The teacher is bringing to conscious awareness, making explicit, the patterns which connect.

ACT ONE Scene Two

The Action Slows

It is about 9.40 a.m. when this discussion finishes. Mrs Brown then announces that it is time for silent reading. About three-quarters of the children immediately move back to the desks and tables. Most of them take books from their desks or from their bags. These books all seem to have bookmarks protruding from them. Some begin reading while at their desks. Others move to the floor at the side or front of the room and settle down there. The other quarter move to the bookshelves situated at the side of the room and begin selecting books. Within five minutes all are seated somewhere with a book, some with two. A deep hush settles over the room and everyone, including Mrs Brown, appears to be deeply engaged with a book. If one took a quick survey of what was being read by whom during this period, the following picture would emerge.

Slavika	Beverley Cleary "Ralph S Mouse" Last Thursday - p.99
Doug	Garfield "The All Round Sports Star" Started today
Thien	Garfield "The Irresistible" Started today
Leann	Enid Blyton "Secret and Win Through" Started Friday - p.26
Steve	"Garfield Weighs In" Thursday - about 3/4 through
Lee-Minh	Margaret Mahy "The Chewing Gum Rescue" Started today - p.9
Keith	Roald Dahl "Fantastic Mr Fox" Started last Tuesday
Jenny	Beverley Cleary "Ramona Quimby Age 8" Started Thursday - p.40
Todd	Robin Klein "Hating Alison Ashley" Started Friday - p.31
Melanie	Francine Pascal "Dangerous Lone" Friday - p.42
Karen-Anne	Enid Blyton "High Adventure" Today - p.63
Jasmina	Graeme Base "My Grandma Lived In Gooligulch" Today - about 4 poems
Paul	Brian Wildsmith "Daisy" Began/finished in one day
Janelle	"TV Adventures of Worzel Gummidge" One week ago - p.50
Michael	Spiders/Insects - ABC book Started today - p.50
Amanda	Robin Klein "Hating Alison Ashley" Friday - p.42
John	Osman White "The Super Roo of Mungalongaloo" Started Friday - p.36
Adrian	3001 jokes. Flipped through Two weeks - dips into it every now & then
Chelsea	"Third Margaret Mahy Storybook" 5th book she's on today
Peter	Australian Pictures Started today - p.37
Dana	Robin Klein "Separate Places" Started today - p.17
Danielle	Robin Klein "Don't Tell Lucy" Started today - 3 pp read other stories another day
Narelle	Santa Claus More than ½

The hush which has settled on the room will last for about ten minutes before one or two children stand and quietly move to the bookshelves to exchange their books. From now on, a trickle of children will do the same thing. The majority, however, will stay in their seats or on the floor and continue reading the original book which they chose. Apart from a few stretches, yawns, shifts of weight on chairs and an occasional whisper to share part of a book, the hush period will continue for about twenty minutes.

Notes on the script (c) Scene 2

Although the action seems to have slowed right down, the conditions of natural learning are strongly evident, some more obvious than others. The behaviour of the children in both selecting books and reading them silently is eloquent evidence of the power of expectations and teacher demonstration working together. The duration of the hush time is an indication of the degree of engagement with text. The need to choose a book to engage with constitutes a further opportunity to take responsibility, i.e. to practice making decisions about learning. The duration of deep engagement with text is the opportunity to employ and use one's burgeoning reading power. Furthermore, every second of deep engagement with text is also adding to the degree to which the setting provides visual immersion in print.

ACT ONE Scene Three

The Action Quickens — The Plot Thickens

At 10 a.m. Mrs Brown announces:

"I want the Tuesday group near my reading chair. The rest of you can continue with your elective activities. Those of you who wish to participate in the sharing, make sure you get your name on the list. We'll have a sharing time about one hour from now."

This appears to be the signal for a change in the rhythm of activity in the class. To an uninformed observer it would seem that the children suddenly start moving in all directions at once. The noise level increases. Children begin moving around the room, many of the carrying large sheets of paper. Others move to the 'Activity Box' and start looking through the envelopes which it contains. Some form into twos and threes and begin reading aloud to each other from pieces of paper which appear to be covered with their own handwriting. Some simply continue reading from the book they had in silent reading time, seemingly oblivious to what's happening around them. Others seem to be working from a specially prepared stencil which is labelled 'General Knowledge Quiz', occasionally wandering out to the reference section of the bookshelves and selecting specific volumes from the set of encyclopaedias which are there, or thumbing through a dictionary or an atlas. A small group of about seven are seated around Mrs Brown's chair. Mrs Brown sits down and speaks to the whole class.

"While I'm talking with the Tuesday group I don't expect to be disturbed. The rest of you should be working on your contracts. You can elect to complete or work on any part of the contract which you chose. All of the material and resources which you need are in the room. You are free to use any of these or you may ask each other to assist you with the processes you need to use to get through any task. You all know how to conference with each other and assist each other with your writing and any other tasks which you need to complete in order to get your contract finished on time. Before you feel the need to ask me for help you should exhaust all other avenues for help. Once I have the Tuesday group started on the special activity I've prepared for them, then I'll be free to help anyone who needs it. I'll also want to check anything that you think is finished. Remember, before you decide to go public with any activity that forms part of your contract you must share what you've done with me. I expect that most of you will need to talk with others in the classroom. All I ask is that you keep the noise level within reasonable limits. No group should be so noisy that they disturb or prevent anyone else from thinking or working on their contracts."

Mrs Brown then turns her attention to the group of seven seated around her and says:

"I've got a sequencing task which I want you to complete cooperatively today. I've taken a chapter from that Colin Thiele book we read a couple of weeks ago and made a number of photocopies of it. I stuck these copies onto stiff cardboard and I've cut them up into chunks of meaning. Some are a paragraph long, some are a few sentences long. I've mixed them all up and I want you to try to put the pieces back together in the correct sequence. Do it silently first and then share and compare your attempts. Remember, don't share and compare until you've all had a go by yourselves. Only then should you discuss and change your original attempt. When you've finished, Cindy can get the book and you can compare your attempt with the original. I'll be back in about twenty minutes and I expect you to be ready to discuss with me your experiences at putting this piece of text back together."

She then hands each child a bundle of cut-up chunks of the text and they move to spaces on the floor and begin reading and sorting, moving pieces of text around like pieces of a jigsaw puzzle as they read, re-read, check and shuffle.

Mrs Brown then stands, moves to her table on the other side of the room and picks up a small notebook which is entitled 'Observations'. She begins to move around the room, interacting with various members of the class who are engaged in their elective activities. Typically, the interactions she has with each child are short, averaging between 45 seconds and a minute. Occasionally she will spend up to three minutes with the same child or group of children. This is, however, rare. As she moves around she occasionally writes something in the notebook that she carries.

The interactions she has with the children fall into two broad categories. Those she initiates and those which the children initiate with her. Whether initiated by her or by a child, there is a similarity about all of the interactions which occur. Here is a typical example:

> **Mrs Brown:** "What are you working on, Jenny?" (Variations of this opening gambit are many, e.g. "What are you supposed to be doing?" "What are you trying to do?" "What part of your contract are you working on?" The purpose appears to be to make the child clarify his or her intent as specifically as possible.)
>
> **Jenny:** "I'm trying to do my special author project. I've written a draft of what I want to go on my Roald Dahl poster."
>
> **Mrs Brown:** "Read it to me."

Jenny responds and reads her draft to Mrs Brown. It's obvious that Jenny has a long way to go. There are any number of areas of her draft that still need work and possibly she needs help in coping with some of them.

Roald Dahls 1.234

The B.F.G, Fantastic m.r
fox, The Twits, Charlie
and the choclate factory,
Charlie and the meat Glass
ellevator, Danny the champion
Of The wo uld, Goerces
Marvolous medicene.
I have read the Twits
and goerces marvalous-
medicene

This is one of
roald dahls charack
Mr,5Twitshe had r
ugly thoughts and s
Got ugly. He Driscribe
His characters well?

Mrs Brown: "What do you want the people who read your poster to know about Roald Dahl, Jenny?"

Jenny looks thoughtful for a few seconds and then replies:

Jenny: "I want them to know what some of the books are that he's written and that he writes about funny events and describes people like Mrs Pratchett and that he's funny and makes you laugh."

Mrs Brown: "Well, you've got the list okay but have you told your reader about the events and characters he writes about?"

Jenny (with some hint of concern in her voice): "Haven't I done it right? What should I do?"

Mrs Brown: "What do you want to do?"

Jenny: "What I said before."

Mrs Brown: "You said that you'd like to tell your reader about some of the funny situations Roald Dahl writes about and some of the characters in his books, didn't you?"

Jenny: "Yes."

Mrs Brown: "Well, tell me about some of them."

Jenny begins to recount some of the events from some of the books she's read, giving detailed accounts of what she means. Mrs Brown listens and nods at the appropriate moments.

> **Mrs Brown:** "Go and write some of those details down on your draft before you forget them and then ask Melissa to listen to what you've written. See if she thinks it's clear. Ask her to help you think of a heading you might use on that section of the poster, a heading that summarises what you're telling your reader."
>
> **Jenny:** "You mean like 'Why I like Roald Dahl's books'?"
>
> **Mrs Brown:** "Yes."

Although on the surface each interaction which Mrs Brown has with each child or group of children during this time is unique, novel and fresh, the underlying structure of each possesses a degree of similarity which is not coincidental. The figure on page 121 sums up the main features of this structure.

For twenty minutes or so, Mrs Brown roves the room interacting with about ten or twelve children, occasionally making notes in her notebook. The purpose of the interactions are wide and varied but essentially they are all concerned with some aspect of the various activities which make up the children's contract in language. In one or two of these Mrs Brown expresses displeasure at what the child has (or hasn't) done. Todd, one of the more able children in the class, obviously has not met the expectation she had for him. She says quite tersely:

> "Todd, you've been wasting your time. You should have done much more than that. Furthermore, its quality simply isn't good enough. I won't accept that from you. Now settle down and get on with the job."

On the other hand, she treats another boy, who has done far less work of much lower quality than Todd's, very differently. Jesse, who cannot read much above Grade 1 level, is struggling with part of his contract, namely 'a piece of quality writing'. Jesse's piece of 'quality writing' is a drawing of the local camping ground's car park with the jetty where he fishes clearly labelled and a simple sentence written underneath. Mrs Brown enthuses about the fact that Jesse has managed to get a sentence written which he can read back to her.

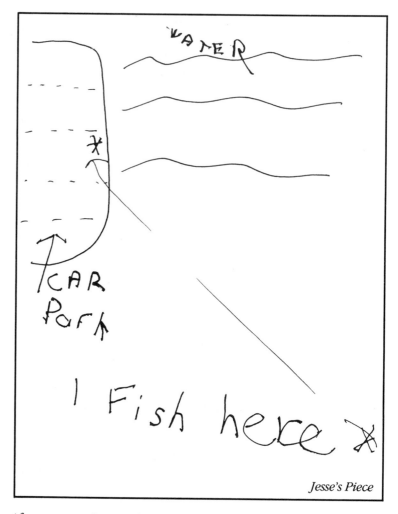

Jesse's Piece

After twenty minutes Mrs Brown moves back to the Tuesday group, who by this time have almost finished comparing their attempts at reassembling the text with the original chapter. They are reading both the original and each other's, and find many points where their reconstruction of the text is not identical with the original, and they are debating whether or not theirs, while different, is still sensible and meaningful. When the group has finished checking, Mrs Brown begins discussing the experience with them.

It is interesting to note that while she spends some time adjudicating whether or not one particular arrangement is semantically acceptable, although it varies from the original text, she seems to spend most of the discussion time getting the children to reflect on the cues they used to help them re-sequence the text, and the strategies they used to solve their sequencing problems. They share these reflections with each other and with her. Mrs Brown uses the opportunity to describe the cues that she uses when trying to read a difficult book and demonstrates very quickly her favourite strategy — going back to the beginning of the sentence and taking a running jump at it. She spends about ten minutes with the Tuesday group, pulling together all the strategies and cues which they have used during the task and does a quick oral summary for them. She then tells them to use the rest of the time available to continue with their elective activities, reminding them that the contract is due in a few weeks.

For the next twenty minutes or so, Mrs Brown continues to rove the room, interacting with children both individually and in small groups. These interactions are sometimes as short as ten or fifteen seconds, or as long as three minutes. About half of them are initiated by her, the rest by the children. She frequently stops and writes something in her notebook before moving on to the next interaction. While these interactions are taking place, the rest of the class appears to engage in a range of individual and group activities. There is a constant buzz of conversation and constant movement throughout the room. A casual observer, if asked to describe what was happening, would probably say something like this:

There were children reading books while seated at their desks or on the floor. Others appeared to be writing, either on loose pages or in a book of some kind. Some of those writing were obviously not taking any care with the neatness and/or appearance of their work, writing quickly and crossing out with big, untidy strokes, stopping every now and then to suck the end of their pens and stare into space, or to read whatever they'd written to someone else.

Others, however, seemed to be taking a great deal of care with whatever they were writing and were obviously copying from a much marked and edited piece of paper. Others were in groups of twos or threes, collaborating on some task. This required them to engage in a whole range of language behaviours including reading and writing, listening to each other and persuading each other about some point of view. They sketched rough outlines of shapes or letters on large sheets of paper or cardboard and sometimes slipped away to the reference section of the bookshelves, returning with something written hastily on a small slip of paper. Two were at the computer; one at the keyboard listening to the other who read from a piece of paper. The one at the keyboard was obviously keying in what was being read. The class was a buzz of noise but not the kind of noise which disturbs or distracts. Amid all of this the teacher carried out a series of conversations with children as she moved constantly around the room, sometimes stopping to write something in the notebook that she was carrying.

Notes on the script (c) Scene 3

While on the surface this a very different scenario, the 'deep structure' of the context remains essentially the same. The action and pace may have changed dramatically but the underlying theory has remained constant. Only the emphasis has shifted. During this segment of the session the responsibility condition comes to the fore. Four-fifths of the learners in the classroom, i.e. those who are not in the Tuesday group, must choose from a number of options what they will spend the next hour doing. They are faced with the task of keeping in mind the overall set of expectations with respect to their contract. At the same time, they balance this against the time which they have left to meet deadlines and the range of activities they can select from in order to meet the conditions of the contract.

Once they make this decision they will then engage in a series of text-making activities which will give them the opportunity to employ and practise their developing skills and knowledge. They give and receive advice and in so doing either make explicit and have made explicit for them a range of concepts and processes about using language to create texts which serve specific purposes. They will give and receive responses about the appropriateness of their attempts to use language for specific purposes and will face the inevitable consequences of discovering that what they intended didn't quite achieve its desired result. In other words, they will find out how their approximations compare with the model that they were trying to emulate.

They know that if their teacher initiates an interaction with them that she will expect them to try to emulate the processes she continually demonstrates in other parts of the session. They will have to clarify their intent, justify their responses and make explicit the patterns which connect. They also know that their attempts to do this, if authentic and within the range of expectations of their teacher, will be accepted without any strings attached. They know they will not be demeaned, denigrated or hurt for 'having a go'. They also know (as Todd found out) that if they do not meet her expectations they will find out about the hard edge which expectations can have. While these interactions are taking place, they will be receiving demonstrations of how questions are asked, how help is given and how responses are made.

These models will be engaged with and will be evident in their later behaviour with each other.

The Tuesday group is freed from the necessity of making a decision about what they will engage with. This is in keeping with the notion that while children are encouraged to take responsibility for decision-making, they cannot make all the decisions. Teachers must make some, particularly those concerned with what will and will not be engaged with. However, within the short time that the teacher works with that group there are a multiplicity of demonstrations given about reading, the processes of reading, the explicit knowledge about the way readers read and the ways in which texts work. There is also further immersion in both visual and aural texts.

While the pace, actions and events are different, the deep learning structure of the scene remains constant and consistent.

ACT ONE Scene Four

The Last Scene

At about 10.55 a.m. Mrs Brown stops moving around the room and interacting with the children of her class. She announces, "It's time for sharing. We'll begin in two minutes."

This is the signal for all of the children to cease whatever they're doing and engage in what could be best described as packing-up behaviour. They put papers into folders, put folders and books into tubs and place them on the shelves which line the walls of the room. They pack pens, pencils and rulers into pencil cases and place them in the small shelves under their desks. They then move to the area that they had occupied earlier when Mrs Brown read to them from *Tom's Midnight Garden*.

However, it is Vanessa who occupies the chair that Mrs Brown used earlier. Mrs Brown sits on a child's chair at the edge of the outer circle of children. All eyes are on Vanessa, who announces, "It's now sharing time. Neil is first to share. Are you ready, Neil?"

Neil moves to the front of the group, just beside Vanessa, with a book in his hand. He begins to talk to the group.

Neil:	Well I read this book called "Life Points" and it's about how everyone dies. It tells people you're not the only one who dies and you don't die straight away. It goes, "There is a beginning and an ending for everything that is alive. In between is living" and then it goes on that all around us everywhere beginnings and endings are going on all the time, and then living in between is true for all things 'For ??, for people, for birds, for trees, for animals, even for the tiniest insect" and then it goes on with illustrations (shows illustrations). The book was written by Brian Mellany (?) and the illustrations were by Robert ??. The blurb on the back is pretty good too. It says "There is a beginning and an

ending to everything that is alive. In between is lifetime. It is the same for people as it is for plants, animals and even for the tiniest insects. Now lifetimes are important for everyone because it helps us to remember to understand to explain that dying is as much a part of living as being born. Any questions?

Paul: Who made you want to read that book?

Neil: Well, when Mrs Brown or Mrs Green, I can't remember, came and they read it and it sounded pretty good and I liked the illustrations so I picked it up to have a look at it.

Cindy: ????? *(Indecipherable)*

Neil: A little bit. Not really it says "even for the tiniest insects" a few times. Doesn't say it a lot.

Tracey: Did you learn anything you didn't know?

Neil: No, not really.

Paul: What did you like about it?

Neil: The illustrations and the way it says it, because you hear people saying you're going to die and you're going to suffer and in here it says you're going to die at some time in your life and it just shows, for the animals, how you might die.

Lou: Does it explain it really good? Like how you die.

Neil: Yeah.

Renee: What did you find the most interesting thing?

Neil: Well probably the part that says "It is the same for people as it is for plants, for birds, for trees, even for the tiniest insect."

Paul: What is it on the front cover?

Neil: Just a sort of swamp creature.

             [General cry of "Alligator"]

Neil: It's not an alligator.

Paul: When Mrs Brown read it she said that it would explain to little kids not to be scared about dying. Do you think that it did a good job?

Neil: Probably, yeah. If they hear someone say about dying like you catch a disease or something they might panic. Any more?

154

After Neil has finished his sharing, Melissa shares a draft of a report she's writing about the antagonism between Henry Lawson and Banjo Patterson and how it relates to the views that each held about life in the city and life in the bush. It's an early draft and she receives lots of questions which are variations of those Mrs Brown asks. For example, 'What are you trying to do?' (clarification of intent). Melissa also receives some advice on parts of her text that are difficult to understand. Mrs Brown waits until the children have ceased commenting then praises Melissa's attempt to deal with such a difficult comparison. She then asks Melissa, 'Where did you get the idea that they were antagonistic towards each other?' Melissa reveals that Mrs Brown had directed her to read some back copies of the Bulletin which were at the local library and that she'd got the idea from there.

Three other children get an opportunity to share before the bell rings for morning recess. One retells a story she'd completed during SSR time and fields about five questions from the audience. Tony shares a piece of writing he's working on and receives some criticism that parts of it are confusing because he has left some detail out. Renae and Shannon share an activity from the Language Activity Box which they've completed. Mrs Brown usually waits until the children have had their say before commenting on, extending, probing, seeking justification, asking for an example or demonstrating something related to the sharing which has taken place. When the bell rings, Vanessa thanks the sharers and the class moves out to morning recess.

Notes on the script (d) The Last Scene

Again the action and the events change but the learning model remains the same. The threads of the conditions of learning described in Chapter 4 can be recognised in the tapestry which unfolds in the sharing session. For example, the session provides a multiplicity of demonstrations of how to present orally to an audience of interested peers. The questions modelled by Mrs Brown in other scenes can be employed and practised here. The context is a friendly, supportive one which expects volunteers to be respected for having a go. Although the decision about when to volunteer is left to the individual learner, the expectation is that sooner or later everyone will volunteer. This expectation ensures that engagement with the demonstrations which are being given is maximised. The session provides a forum for making explicit how others interpret and create text.

8

Making Connections I: Understanding Reading

Introduction

In the previous chapter we observed one teacher's attempt to implement the theory of natural learning in her classroom. While it was obvious that the teacher had a thorough understanding of the principles of natural learning as they were outlined in the earlier chapters, it should be clear to most readers that this was not all she knew. **The teacher also had a very thorough understanding of reading and writing and how they related to each other and to the development of literacy.**

In order to make what I have called 'natural learning' work, it is imperative that such connections are made. This is because I believe that teachers who are equipped with a robust theory of learning and a thorough understanding of the domain of concern that they are helping learners learn about are then in a strong position when it comes to planning the programme of **demonstrations** (artifacts and actions) and the kinds of **immersion** which are most appropriate for their pupils. Furthermore, they are able to offer the most appropriate forms of **response**, because they are aware of the kinds of **approximations** that learners are likely to make. In short, they are better equipped to ensure that the principles of learning can be shaped to fit the contours of whatever it is that is being learned.

What Do Teachers Need to Know about Reading and Writing?

Because of the important roles that reading and writing play in the acquisition and development of literacy, it is important that teachers also know about reading and writing.

In my opinion, there are at least three questions about reading and writing that teachers should be able to answer with confidence:

(i) What is reading and/or writing? Without an unambiguous definition of what it is one is talking about when one uses these terms, all kinds of confusions can occur. By reading, do teachers mean the act of pronouncing words accurately? Do they mean a score on a standardised test? Do they mean what learners do on worksheets? By 'writing', do they mean what is done in examinations? Do they mean studying the conventions of spelling, punctuation and grammar? Do they mean being creative? Do they mean writing stories? Do they mean being able to communicate effectively? Teachers need to know precisely what it is that they are talking about when they refer to the acts of reading and writing.

(ii) How does reading/writing happen? I strongly believe that as well as understanding how learning happens, effective teachers of literacy also need to know how reading happens, how writing happens and how some of the accoutrements of writing, such as spelling, happen. By 'happens' I mean the processes and knowledge which learners need to control to be effective readers/writers. I am not going to attempt to define what effective reading and writing is. This will emerge as the text unfolds.

(iii) What have effective readers/writers learned? Why should teachers be explicitly aware of what it is that effective readers/writers have learned before they actually attempt to teach reading/writing? Simply because teachers need to know where their pupils should be heading.

Just as parents have a very good sense of how a finished/graduated/complete talker in their culture behaves, so teachers need to know how the finished/graduated/complete reader/writer should behave, i.e. what he should do and how he should be doing it.

There is another reason why this kind of information is important to the teacher. If teachers can be explicit about the kinds of things that effective readers/writers have learned to do, then they are in a better position to make judgements about what it is they should be demonstrating, what they should be expecting, how they should be responding and the kinds of approximations which can be expected when their charges are just beginning their learning journey. In other words, they need to be able to work back from the finished product (in the sense that someone who can read and write effectively is a finished product) and thus gain some clear understanding of the kinds of things that they should be teaching young learners.

This approach reverses that which is typically applied in courses offered to teachers in training, especially with respect to Special Education or Remedial Education. In these courses, teachers spend a great deal of their time looking at what it is that **ineffective** readers and writers do or can't do. There is a kind of implicit, unwritten agreement that everybody knows what the **good** reader/writer knows and/or does. The problem with this approach is that it is not grounded in what **real** learners reading or writing **real** texts actually do. Rather, it is based on the same kind of reductionist logic that characterises other aspects of learning theory. For example, because it is **logical** that the act of reading or writing can be described as an aggregate of separate skills, it is assumed that **psychologically** it is best learned the same way. A good illustration of this kind of logic is the traditional assertion that those who are really good readers are also good at something called phonics. What is never seriously asserted is that they are good at phonics **because** they are good readers. Before any assertions can be made about ineffective or underdeveloped reading/writing, I would argue that we need to begin with the other end of the spectrum — what is it that the effective reader/writer has learned to do?

The following delineates what it is about reading/writing that I believe teachers should know and understand if they are going to apply the principles of natural learning appropriately to literacy acquisition.

What Is Reading?

My answer to this question is a simple one.

Reading is comprehension.

By this I mean that the end result of any act of engagement with text **must be** comprehension of the meanings which the author of the text originally encoded. In fact, I would assert that unless comprehension of the meanings which the author originally constructed does take place, then one would be hard put to argue that an act of reading has occurred. For comprehension to occur, readers must first construct a text (a meaningful message) inside their heads. The effectiveness of any act of reading thus becomes a function of the degree to which the meanings in the text constructed by the reader matches the meanings which the author of the text intended. The higher the degree of similarity of meaning between the two texts (the author's and the reader's), the more effective the reading has been. This does not mean that the reader must understand exactly and precisely what the author of the text originally intended. Such photographic reconstruction is neither physiologically nor psychologically possible. All that can be hoped for is an approximation, often a very close approximation, to the meanings that the author intended. The reasons for this are complex and intricate and this is not the appropriate arena for delving into them. When my students want to convince me that they've read a particular text that I've set ('read' in the sense of 'comprehended'), I handle it thus. If they can retell it in ways that capture what I consider to be the relevant gist, details, points and arguments, I will consider that they have read it. Of course, some will read it better than others, for reasons which will become obvious when we begin to explore the questions of how reading works. For our purposes it is sufficient to stay with what at first looks to be a rather simplistic definition of reading: **Reading is comprehension.**

Okay, but isn't that a rather too simplistic definition?

Sometimes, when I make this rather simple statement to teachers, student teachers or teacher educator colleagues, I am accused of being superficial, simplistic, banal, trivial or glib. I disagree. There are some very important, complex, deep and non-trivial ramifications which flow from such a simple definition. Let me explain. Here is a text written in English orthography:

> *Pokarekare ana*
> *Nga wai o Rotorua*
> *Whiti atu koe hine*
> *Marino ane e.*
>
> *E hine e*
> *Hoki mai ra*
> *Ka mate ahau*
> *I te aroha e.*

In order to demonstrate what I mean about reading not having taken place unless comprehension has also occurred, I often asked fluent adult readers (teachers and parents) to 'read' out loud, this piece of text. (Once a group of 50 or so male school inspectors sang it for me, in beautiful baritone voices.) When the audience has finished 'reading' the text out loud, I usually call for volunteers to demonstrate to everyone that they have truly 'read' this piece by displaying the depth of their comprehension. I invite them to do this by doing either an oral or written retelling of the meanings which the author of the words of the song encoded. Very rarely, outside of New Zealand, have many people who have successfully pronounced the words using their knowledge of the phonemic structure of English (phonics), been able to do even a simple retelling of the meanings in the song. I then usually inform them that, in my opinion, they can't claim to have 'read' this piece of text. They can be said to have mouthed the words, or carried out an act of pronunciation, or performed an act of elocution — but in no way can they be said to have 'read' it. Of course, when I do this to large groups there are some who want to argue that it is an unfair test because 'it's a foreign language to most of us. How could we be expected to comprehend it when we don't know the language in the first place?'

They are, of course, absolutely justified in making such a claim. The point I try to make with them is that we should not confuse what they did, i.e. pronounce words, with the act of reading. I try to point out to them that what they did, i.e. pronounce words, is not very different from what many children are having demonstrated to them in school when they are asked to do things which are usually called 'reading' but which are devoid of meaning.

It should be noted that my definition of reading is at variance with some writers in the field. For example, in 1955, Rudolf Flesch, the author of an extremely popular book, *Why Johnny Can't Read,* wrote:

> *Many years ago when I was about fifteen, I took a semester's course in Czech; I have since forgotten everything about the language itself but I still remember how the letters are pronounced, plus the simple rule that all words have the accent on the first syllable. Armed with this knowledge I once surprised a native of Prague by reading aloud from a Czech newspaper. "Oh, you know Czech?" he asked. "No, I don't understand a word of it," I answered. "I can only read it."*

My only response to such a statement is that it seems to me to be extremely illogical. I can see no point in engaging with text other than to construct the message which has been encoded by the author. Reading in order **not** to comprehend simply doesn't make sense.

How Does Reading Happen?

If it can be agreed that the end result of interacting with a text (reading) should be comprehension, then it follows that teachers should understand and appreciate how comprehension occurs, i.e. how meaning is constructed from pieces of text. Let me sensitise you to some of the issues involved in comprehension by asking you to reflect upon your own attempts to comprehend some written text. I want you to examine carefully the text set out in the box below.

> Richmond was in dire straits against St Kilda. The opening pair who had been stroking the ball with beautiful fluency on past occasions were both out for ducks. Once again the new ball pair had broken through. Then Smith turned on surprising pace and, moving the ball off the seam, beat Mazaz twice in one over. Inverarity viciously pulled Brown into the gully but was sent retiring to the pavilion by a shooter from Cox.
>
> Jones in slips and Chappell at silly mid on were superb, and Daniel bowled a maiden over in his first spell. Yallop took his toll with three towering sixes but Thompson had little to do in the covers.
>
> Grant was dismissed with a beautiful yorker and Jones went from a brute of a ball. Wood was disappointing. The way he hung his bat out to the lean-gutted Croft was a nasty shock. The rout ended when McArdle dived at silly leg and the cry of 'How's that!' echoed across the pitch.[1]

Let me now ask you to answer, as honestly as possible, the following questions:

1. Apart from proper nouns (names of person/places) how many of the words in this text are totally new print items. That is, you've never seen them in print before. (Please note I'm **not** asking whether you've seen them used with these particular meanings before. I'm asking whether you've ever seen them in print with any kind of meaning before.)
2. How many of the words, apart from proper nouns, do you need help with in pronouncing?
3. How many words could you **not** use in a sentence of some kind? (For example, 'yorker' — he's a New Yorker.)
4. Can you comprehend the text, i.e. do a retelling which would convince me that you understood what the text was about?

---

[1] This text has been taken from an Australian newspaper. A few names have been altered to make it more relevant to modern cricket.

Typically, when I ask Australian audiences to read this text and answer these questions, the responses are similar. Typically, the first three questions are answered thus: every word (excluding proper nouns) has been seen in print before, every word can be pronounced, and every word can be used in a sentence of some kind. When question four is discussed, (Can you comprehend the text?), it is not unusual for more than 50% of the audience (in some cases, 100% if the audience is all women) to admit that very little comprehension has taken place.

Why? Does it mean that these people have a reading problem? If I were to give them some intense word recognition/flash card drill on the words in the text, would it improve their comprehension? What about if I followed word recognition practice with some super-effective phonic drill? Would that help their comprehension? What if I gave them a dictionary? When I ask these questions of those who can't comprehend the text, they shake their heads. The reasons for their lack of comprehension of this particular text go far beyond simplistic explanations about word recognition, phonic ability or vocabulary — although Flesch would argue that they had 'read' the text.

Well, if it's not a word recognition problem, a phonic problem or a vocabulary (in the pure dictionary sense) problem, why can't they comprehend this text?

As you processed the text above at least one thing should have become obvious to you. It is this. As a reader, if you are to understand what the writer of that piece intends you to understand, you must go beyond the actual words that have been written in the text. You must make connections between statements. You must fill in many communicative gaps that have been left in the discourse. What sport is being played? What's an opening pair? What's a new ball pair? What did they break through? What was Daniel doing to a maiden? What was Thompson doing in covers? If the connections and gap-filling are done correctly then you have a very good chance of comprehending what the author intended. On the other hand, if you are unable to make these connections, then comprehension will be incomplete and distorted. In the text above, the connections which have to be made are multitudinous. Among other things, one has to know that Richmond and St Kilda are cricket teams, that cricket is played in a certain way with particular objectives, rules, rituals, conventions and so on.

This process of constructing relations (making connections) between events is called **inferencing**. It is a central process in all language comprehension and if it does not occur, or occurs wrongly, then comprehension will be negatively affected. The ability to make the kinds of inferences that are necessary for comprehension to occur is **not** an esoteric skill that needs to be learned or taught. Inferencing is what the brain does naturally to make discourse intelligible and communication possible. Inferencing is both natural and necessary because of the way discourse is structured. In all discourse only some of the relations between the things the discourse is about are explicit in the surface features of the message. Most of the important relations are implicit and must be inferred by the reader or the listener. If this were not the case, and every detail had to be included in the surface of the message, then discourse would become extremely boring, long-winded and probably impossible. If readers or listeners were designed so that this ability to inference did not occur, then every part of the message would need to be particularised and detailed. All the presuppositions we typically make when reconstructing a message would need to be specifically referred to. A simple statement like, "I got up this morning" would have to be stated something like this.

> "First I opened my eyes, then I moved my left leg, than my right leg, then my left leg again, then my right leg again. I put my right foot on the floor, then my left foot . . . "

Thankfully, because the human brain is designed to fill in (inference), it is not necessary for all this trivial detail to be in the signal. We know from our previous experiences of getting up in the morning that we have to open our eyes and generally carry out a host of microscopic movements in order to get up. Because the phrase 'getting up in the morning' encapsulates all these actions and movements the necessity for particularising everything is removed.

Notwithstanding the naturalness of the inferencing process, it is obvious that not everybody comprehends with the same degree of effectiveness. Some comprehenders are obviously more effective than others. what factors would predispose some comprehenders to be better than others? Why do some people seem to be better at understanding what they read? One of the major factors on which successful inferencing seems to depend is the knowledge of the world and the relations that exist between entities in the world. Typically, those 'readers' who are not cricket lovers find the text incomprehensible.

Successful comprehension, it seems, occurs when the comprehender has sufficient knowledge of the topic of discourse to fill in all the gaps between the intended meaning and the surface features of the signal. Less successful comprehension occurs when the reader does not have enough real world knowledge to make the inferences that fill the gaps. This is a long-winded way of saying that **when engaged in reading, comprehension depends on the reader being able to construct a text which matches what the author of that particular text intended. Constructing a text depends in turn upon the reader** being able to bring to bear a certain body of knowledge and range of skills including semantic knowledge, syntactic knowledge, graphophonic knowledge, process knowledge and certain procedural skills.

In what follows, these kinds of knowledge and skills are explored in more detail.

But what about those learners who do know about cricket but still can't read that text?

It is all very well to argue that one of the prerequisites of effective reading of any text is that the reader must be familiar with the semantic and syntactic aspects of it. But one should then not assume that that is all that is involved. Those of us who've taught children can easily recall any number who are cricket (or football or baseball, etc.) afficionados, who know the game and the vocabulary of the game and who can talk about the game using the same language and metaphors as the experts, yet who, when confronted with the written form of this language are reduced to the level of a non-reader. No matter how hard they try they cannot seem to construct any meanings from the text. If it's not lack of familiarity with the semantic or syntactic aspects of the text that is preventing them from reading (understanding) it, what then is the cause of their inability to read?

The answer seems obvious. As well as needing prior knowledge, effective readers must need some other kind of knowledge and/or skill which enables them to construct the meanings of the text. I want to suggest that this other kind of skill/knowledge is associated with the processes which underlie the act of effective reading.

What Are the Processes Involved which Underlie Effective Reading?

a) Identifying the processes involved in reading.

The processes which underlie effective reading are difficult to get at for a number of reasons. Firstly, whatever processing is taking place is covert. It takes place under the scalp or inside the head. With respect to the most common kind of reading (silent reading) there is very little which is overtly visible. I've spent a good portion of the last few years of my life observing children engaged in the act of silent reading and it's virtually impossible to observe much beyond some very molar behaviours such as that every so often they turn the page, look up, gaze around for a few seconds and the re-engage with the text. There seems to be a limit to the insights that can be gained from observing readers engaged in the act of silent reading.

A second factor that makes getting at the processes involved in effective reading difficult is this — effective silent reading is an automatic, unconscious process, which is rarely thought about or reflected upon by those who are capable of doing it. They merely take it for granted, in much the same way that they take using the oral form of the language for granted. Little wonder that the precise nature of what it is that the good reader actually does as he interacts with text is not well-known.

b) Getting inside readers' heads

There are, however, some useful things known about the processes which underlie reading. Strangely enough, we've learned about them from the errors or miscues or deviations from the actual text which readers make when they read out loud. Because of the work of researchers like Kenneth Goodman and many of his students and colleagues, we have come to realise that the deviations which readers make when they read aloud can be used as windows, albeit rather opaque ones, through which we can observe what takes place inside a reader's head when engaged in the act of reading. Let me try to explain using a simple example.

Imagine that two children of similar ability and background are reading the same piece of text — a story about cowboys and Indians. Let us also imagine that both of them are about nine years of age and are in Grade 4 and that both have been given these instructions by their teacher:

> "I want you to read this story out loud. I want you to pay attention to the things which happen in the story because when you finish reading I'm going to ask you to tell me about it. I'm just going to listen. If you come to something you don't know, just do the best you can. Don't spend too long on things you don't know. Just do the best you can."

Let us also imagine that the children both read the piece. One of the things we notice is that neither of them gives a perfect rendition of the text. They both seem to make lots of 'mistakes', in that they omit words that are part of the text, or they substitute one word for another, sometimes correcting this substitution and sometimes not.

Now let us imagine that about halfway through this story there is this sentence:

The cowboy jumped onto his horse and rode away.

Child number 1 deviates from the text when he gets to the word horse. He substitutes another word for it. He reads:

The cowboy jumped onto his *bose* and rode away.

By some strange coincidence the second reader deviates at exactly the same word. By another coincidence, his deviation is also a substitution. He reads:

The cowboy jumped onto his *mustang* and rode away.

Let us stretch our imagination just a little further for the sake of illustrating a point. Firstly, let us also pretend that, by some enormous coincidence, both of these readers had each made another 99 deviations throughout the story so that each had made exactly 100 so-called 'errors'. Finally, let us assume that each of them had a large proportion of the same type of 'error' sprinkled throughout their oral reading. That is, child 1 made HOSE—HORSE substitutions while child 2 made MUSTANG—HORSE substitutions.

Many teachers (and non-teachers) might regard the deviations as 'errors' and assume that since both readers made exactly 100, that they are readers who are about equal in reading ability. Some may even argue that neither are very effective readers because of the fact that they made so many 'errors'. (I have put quotation marks around 'errors' because I do not consider them errors in the sense that they are wrong. Some are quite correct in terms of meaning, e.g. mustang.)

We need to ask ourselves what these errors mean. What causes them? Are they merely random events which have no deep-seated causes at all? Are they the result of inattention? Laziness? Sheer bloody-mindedness on the part of the reader? Do they reflect a momentary aberration of the reader's visual system? Do they occur because the reader is tired? While these are appealing explanations which are often offered to explain away errors such as these, they are not only simplistic, they are quite invalid.

Why?

There are two things that become obvious when one observes large numbers of readers engaged in oral reading under similar conditions to those described above. Firstly, all readers, when asked to read out loud, unless they are reading something which is extremely simple and familiar, make 'errors'. That is, they deviate from the text in front of their eyes. Even the best of readers. Even those who read the news on the radio or TV are continually making deviations from the printed text which meets their eyes. It happens so frequently with respect to effective readers (those readers who can prove they have comprehended the text by giving a very detailed and carefully composed retelling), that it could be argued that 'effective reading is characterised by deviation from the printed text'! Another way of stating this is to say that errorless reproduction of the precise words which are on the page is not a necessary prerequisite of effective reading.

Furthermore, when one examines them, it becomes obvious that these deviations are not random, haphazard events that occur for trivial reasons like tiredness or inattention. Rather, they are visible instances of what the reader's brain typically does as it proceeds with the task of making meaning from the print in front of the eyes. Typically, they are the result of the reader's reading system being put under just enough strain to bring to the surface those underground, covert, invisible processes that are part of the reading act. In short, they are clues to what the reader is trying to do as he interacts with the print; clues that only become visible (overt) when there is a deviation from how the text actually looks. They also reflect some of the invisible processing strategies that readers must be using when they don't make 'errors', that is, when they don't deviate from the text.

If these assumptions about the origins and status of oral reading deviations (henceforth 'miscues') can be accepted, it becomes obvious that if we could collect enough of them we should be able to get some insights into how readers actually go about the task of constructing meaning from text. Perhaps a simple example will help make this clear.

A closer look at the hypothetical miscues made by two hypothetical readers:

Let us examine the hypothetical deviations made by our hypothetical readers in more detail and see if we can explain them in a rational, sensible way. In other words, let's try to build a theory.

TEXT: The cowboy jumped onto his **horse** and rode away.
CHILD 1: The cowboy jumped onto his **hose** and rode away.
CHILD 2: The cowboy jumped onto his **mustang** and rode away.

What could we say about Child 1's miscue? Let's look at it from the perspective of how close the word *hose* is to the word which should have been read, *horse*. In terms of physical appearance, or what is sometimes called **graphic similarity**, it is very close. One couldn't get much closer in terms of graphic similarity without actually getting *horse*. There's only one letter which is different. On a scale of 1 to 10, I would rate *hose* to be a 9 in terms of the degree of graphic similarity to the intended word.

One can look at closeness of match from another perspective, for example, the sounds involved. How close is the word *hose* to *horse* in terms of the sound segments involved? Shut your eyes so that the graphic shape can't distract you and say each word slowly to yourself a couple of times. There's not much difference, is there? All that is really different is the middle sound. Apart from this minor difference the two words are very similar in terms of the sounds which are involved. So for **phonemic similarity** (degree of similarity between sounds in the word which should have been read and the words which was actually read), on a scale of 10 I'd probably give this miscue an 8 or 9 as well.

How else can we look at this miscue? We've looked at it from the perspective of graphic similarity, we've also looked at it from the perspective of sound or phonemic similarity. How about 'meaning similarity'? After all, I've argued that, as far as I'm concerned, reading is comprehension. How does *hose* compare with *horse* in terms of matching the author's intended meaning — what is sometimes referred to as 'the meaning match'? On a scale of 10, what would we award *hose* for meaning? I give it a 0. *Hose* has no meaning relationship with *horse* at all. In fact it turns the sentence into a meaningless bit of nonsense. Cowboys don't jump onto hoses and ride away! Not in the real world of meaning. If somebody **said** something like this in the course of conversation, we'd be surprised and would probably begin to suspect some kind of joke. We certainly wouldn't accept it as a normal piece of everyday discourse because it conflicts with everything we know about the real world of cowboys and horses and riding. Therefore, we should not be prepared to accept it in the reading context either. So the substitution of *hose* for *horse* deserves a 0 rating in terms of what might be loosely called **meaning match**. Just on these three ways of looking at Child 1's deviations, we could summarise our judgements thus:

Graphic Match   9/10
Phonemic Match   8/10
Meaning Match   0/10

If the majority of the other 99 miscues made by Child 1 were of the same type, it would be reasonable to assert that Child 1 is a reader who is 'good' at making graphic and phonic matches, but not 'good' at getting a meaning match. (What would typically happen to him in most Australian classrooms? He'd be withdrawn and put into a remedial class where most likely he'd be given and intensive programme of . . . you've guessed it . . . phonics and word recognition!)

Let us now carry out the same kind of analysis with Child 2. He also miscues on the word *horse*. He substituted *mustang* for it. In terms of graphic similarity, who would we rate these two words? On a scale of 10 I would rate this as 0. There is absolutely no graphic similarity between the two. What about phonemic similarity? Shut your eyes and say the segments of sound in each word. Again, one would have to rate the degree of similarity as 0. All that each word seems to have in common is an 's' sound but even these occur in quite different parts of the word. What about degree of meaning match? How similar in meaning is the reader's word, *mustang,* to the author's word, *horse?* In terms of the meaning which the reader has stored away in his head as a consequence of interacting with this text, has the concept *mustang* caused him any serious loss of the author's intended meaning? How does *mustang* rate on a scale of 10 in terms of meaning similarity? Personally, I would give it 11! Child 2 is a specialist. His choice of word is more precise than the author's and *mustang* probably describes more accurately what it is that cowboys do, in fact, ride in their day-to-day activities. Thus, in terms of three aspects of the miscue we could summarise Child 2 thus:

Graphic Match	0/10
Phonemic Match	0/10
Meaning Match	11/10

I asked you to pretend for the sake of illustration that both Child 1 and Child 2 each made 100 miscues throughout their oral reading of the stories, and that the majority of these 100 miscues were of the same kind. In other words, Child 1's most common kind of miscue was the *hose/horse* type of miscue, while Child 2's most common miscue was of the *mustang/horse* variety. If this were the case, what does a pattern of miscues like this indicate about each one of these readers? Can we safely assume that each of them are about the same because they both made 100 miscues? Can we say that they are both poor readers because they both made so many miscues? This would presuppose that good reading is errorless reproduction of the precise words on the page.

I want to suggest that patterns of miscues like these enable us to make some very strong inferences about the ways in which each of these two hypothetical readers approach the task of reading. For example, it would be reasonable to argue that Child 1 does not have a meaning focus. If he did, he would not be prepared to tolerate the kind of semantic nonsense that the *hose/horse* substitution creates. Remember, he did it 99 other times throughout his reading. The fact that he made no attempt to correct this substitution suggests that he is not even aware of the face that he has produced semantic nonsense. The only other explanation for his passive acceptance of this kind of gibberish is that he believes that reading is more about getting the next word out than it is about construction of meaningful texts, or, that he is locked into a mode of operating which forces him to both produce and accept semantic nonsense.

This explanation is supported by the fact that this reader's miscues are very high in terms of the degree of physical similarity to the word which the author of the text used. Why are they so similar? It suggests that this reader is putting most of his cognitive effort into the task of achieving close graphic and phonemic matches. Because he believes that reading is about saying words, his major concern is to get the next word out. If one could get inside his head to see what rule or programme was driving his reading behaviour, I would suspect that we'd find something like this operating:

> *There's a word coming up in this sentence that I'm not sure of — that one which is spelled h/o/r/s/e/. My strategy when this occurs is to try to get a word that looks and sounds as much like that word as possible. If in the process of doing this I lose meaning, it really doesn't matter because reading has very little to do with meaning anyway.*

With this kind of rule or programme driving his reading behaviour, he proceeds to attack the unknown word using strategies that help him achieve what it is he thinks should be done, namely, phonic analysis and/or rote recall of words he's seen in the past that look just like the one before him now.

One can infer quite different things about Child 2 *(mustang/horse)*. If the majority of his miscues are of this kind, then it would be reasonable to argue that what he has stored away inside his head as a consequence of reading the story must resemble very much the meanings which the author of the story intended. While he may have stored these meanings away using different vocabulary forms (such as *mustang* for *horse*), it would be reasonable to argue that the pictures he gets in his mind are consistent with those which the original writer of the text had in his mind when composing it. Furthermore, it would be valid to assert that a pattern of miscues such as this, i.e. predominantly *mustang/horse* type miscues, reveals that this reader has a meaning focus, that his major aim when reading is to keep the storyline of the piece of text which he is reading coherent, sensible and within the bounds of meaning that the print setting in which he happens to be operating, demands. If we could get inside his head to find out what kind of programme was driving his reading behaviour, I want to suggest that we would find something like this:

There's a word coming up which I've never seen before and don't recognise. When I get to it, my strategy will be to search for a word that makes the best sense in terms of the storyline that I'm building. If this means I have to sacrifice graphic and/ or phonemic similarity, then so be it. I will not trade off meaning just to get the next word out.

It is obvious that, when interpreted from this perspective, both readers are very different. One, according to the definition I gave earlier, would be perceived to be a good reader. The other would be considered an ineffective reader. Child 2 would be considered to be the effective one. (Remember our definition of reading? **Reading is comprehension.**) If his *mustang/horse* substitution is typical of how he proceeded when reading silently, then there would be no reason to think that he was in any need of help. He apparently has control of the processes that he needs to get a reasonable accurate facsimile of the author's meaning inside his own mind. There is a very strong possibility that his retelling of the text would be good.

The other reader (Child 1) needs help. If his *hose/horse* miscue is typical of how he proceeds when reading silently, then what he is storing away must be meaningless nonsense. When the brain is called upon to made sense of something which is nonsensical, it does one of two things. It imposes sense on it or it opts out. Child 1 has opted out of trying to create meaning. He blithely proceeds to get the next word out without any obvious evidence that he is bothered about monitoring what he's saying. I often speculate how such readers would behave if one talked similar nonsense in their presence. If one is prepared to accept nonsense often enough, it becomes habitual and, ultimately, reading nonsense becomes habitual. One of the characteristics of the brain is that it finds boredom (lack of sense or meaning) aversive and so avoids it. A possible long-term result of such behaviour is that reading becomes something in which you engage only when you have to.

What Have Effective Readers Learned?

This question begs a prior one: 'What is an effective reader?' Asking this question in the company of reading experts is akin to asking 'What is the good life?' or 'What is the meaning of life?' in the company of philosophers. It can be approached from a multiplicity of perspectives and often generates long argument and counter-argument.

I first addressed myself to this question in a project which my colleague, Peter Rousch, directed. *(Rousch & Cambourne, 1978)* We adopted a low-key, naturalistic approach to it. We asked a large number of teachers to rank the children in their classes in order of reading ability. We gave them no precise directions on how they were to do this. When they had ranked the children in their classes, we creamed off those who fell in the top 5% of all the rankings and proceeded to collect as much information as we could about them and how they thought, felt and actually went about reading. We compared what they said, believed, thought and did with respect to reading, with those who fell in the middle and bottom 5% of these rankings. One could say that our definition of the effective reader is anyone who falls in the top 5% of teachers' rankings.

Our reasons for going about it this way were simple and straightforward. We believed that teachers, who are trained professionals and who spend six hours per day, 200 days per year, observing their students engaged in learning and reading are in the best position to make informed judgements about reading behaviour, especially as it relates to school reading. They are not unlike anthropologists who spend sustained periods of time living with tribes or cultures in order to find out what makes them tick. The information they have access to is just as rich and, if interpreted properly, just as credible and trustworthy. It is interesting to note that those teachers who participated used a range of techniques for ranking their children. Some gave a standardised test; some used informal reading inventories; others synthesised all the records that related to any kind of reading behaviour they'd observed during the year and made a judgement about their children's reading ability; some even used what they called 'gut feelings'.

Here's what we found out by asking the children who fell into the top, middle and bottom 5% of these rankings a range of open-ended questions about their attitudes, beliefs and understandings of reading and by analysing their reading behaviour through their retellings and their miscues.

What the effective and ineffective readers know about reading

Effective readers are aware that the purpose of reading anything is to understand it. They demonstrate this focus both directly and indirectly. If, for example, you ask them directly what they focus on when they read, or what it is that good readers do, their replies typically have a meaning focus. "Glen's a good reader 'cos he understands what he reads"; "Joanne's the best reader in our class because when she reads something just once she knows what it's all about", etc.

They confirm this direct focus on meaning in other, less direct ways. If, for example, you ask them to read a text and subsequently retell it, their retellings are quite different from those of less able readers. In a series of research projects which I've carried out over the last few years, one of the things which clearly distinguishes between those whom teachers regard as good and poor readers is the quality of their retellings. Effective readers' retellings are well organised, with evidence of selection and organisation of relevant detail. These retellings typically contain the main points and/or essence of the original text. Often they are characterised by paraphrases which capture the original meanings with different vocabulary.

By contrast, less able readers' retellings are usually lists of unconnected items or events from the original text. They lack coherence and focus. To anyone who does not know the original text, they sound like an incomprehensible maze of disconnected discourse. There is little evidence of effective paraphrase. Rather, there is evidence of unsuccessful rote memorisation of the precise words and phrases used in the original text — only fragments of the original wording occur in the retelling. It is as if these readers have grabbed at isolated bits of the text and tried to commit them to memory. It seems as if good readers not only know that comprehension should be the end product of an act of reading but also that they should work actively and deliberately towards making sense of (comprehending) what it is that they are reading. Furthermore, they are aware when comprehension is not occurring. Less effective readers, as a group, do not have the same focus. Like Child 1, our *hose/horse* reader, they seem to have a quite different focus. They behave in ways that suggest that they don't have the same obsession with meaning and are not nearly as put off when they fail to achieve it. Stated simply, they don't seem to be as completely obsessed with meaning as do their more effective peers.

How Do Effective and Ineffective Readers Process Print?

Here is a summary of research which has attempted to examine the miscues of both effective and less effective readers.

1. All readers, both the effective and the ineffective, make 'errors' or 'miscues' when they attempt to read text aloud.

In some research there is evidence that the actual rate of miscues per hundred words of text does not vary significantly from effective to ineffective readers. If this research accurately reflects what it is that effective readers actually do when engaged in the act of reading, then it appears that making miscues is a normal, perhaps essential, part of the process. Perhaps it is necessary to reassess what is meant by accuracy in reading. Does it mean errorless reproduction of what is on the page? Or does it mean accuracy of meaning, possibly expressed through a different form of words? (Like our *mustang/horse* reader.) The way in which teachers answer this question has important ramification for the way in which the pedagogy of reading is approached.

2. Effective and ineffective readers' miscues are different.

Although both effective and ineffective readers produce miscues when they read, this is where any similarity between them stops. One thing which sets them apart is the nature of the miscues which they produce. The differences between the two groups are quite unambiguous. Effective readers' miscues are mainly of the *mustang/horse* variety. That is, they are miscues which do not cause any serious loss of meaning. They are miscues which not only keep the storyline going, but which also preserve the 'Englishness' of the language, producing sentence structures which do not violate the syntactic structure of English. On the other hand, ineffective readers (those whose retellings do **not** reflect comprehension of the original text) produce miscues which destroy the coherency of the original storyline by producing semantic and/or syntactic nonsense. The *hose/horse* example is a miscue which produces semantic nonsense, but which does not destroy the 'Englishness' of the syntax.[1] Such behaviour reflects a quite different focus — graphic/phonemic similarity at the expense of meaning. In short, behind the miscue behaviour of these two groups of readers there are quite distinct processing strategies.

3. The correction behaviour of effective/ineffective readers is quite different.

While there are some readers who rarely attempt to adjust a miscue, the majority of readers, as they work their way through a text, often engage in some form of correcting behaviour. Typically, this takes the form of backing up and attempting to reprocess the bit of text on which they've miscued. The data from some research indicates that both effective and ineffective readers attempt some form of correction behaviour with about 30% of their miscues. This means that they leave a massive 70% of all their miscues uncorrected. What distinguishes the effective from the ineffective reader is this — the effective readers typically correct only those miscues which cause a loss of meaning. If they judge the storyline not to have been seriously

---

[1] Ineffective readers often produce miscues which destroy the syntactic structure of English as well. A reader who substituted the verb form 'housed' for 'horse' is an example.

compromised, they typically ignore it. Not so with the ineffective readers. Their corrections are not typically based on meaning loss. Rather, they seem to be based on attempts to achieve an even closer graphic and/or phonic match.

4. Effective readers engage in a great deal of prediction while they read.

When one examines effective readers' miscue patterns together with their patterns of correction, it strongly suggests that effective readers are engaging in a particular kind of prediction. Furthermore, when one asks them to comment on their own reading behaviour, they will actually tell you that that is what they are doing. For example, imagine a reader reading a text about going to the beach, in which the following sentence occurs:

I would go to the beach first and then put on my tea.[2]

He proceeds thus:

"I would go to the beach first and then put on my buh... er tea."

When asked why he said 'buh' and then changed it to 'tea', his reply was:

"I was going to say 'bathers' (swimming apparel) but then I saw it was too short for that and it started with a 't'."

This kind of predicting behaviour is evident when one listens to effective readers in action. These predictions are not random guesses. They're based on data which the reader is constantly using, namely the sense of story and the flow of language. The reader used in the example above predicted that 'bathers' was coming up because it fitted in with the scene he was building up in his head (in Australia, one does sometimes put on one's bathers after one arrives at the beach), and it also was a noun which happened to be able to fit into that slot in that particular sentence. Ineffective readers do not predict in the same way. One cannot find many instances of ineffective readers producing miscues which could be explained in terms of a 'predictions-based-on-a-developing-storyline' or 'a-feel-for-the-way-the-language-should-be-flowing' theory.

Furthermore, if one asks them why they make the miscues which they actually produce, they respond in ways which suggest that they

---

[2] In Australia and New Zealand, 'tea' in this context refers to the evening meal. To 'put on tea' means to cook the evening meal.

are **not** predicting in quite the same way as the effective readers do. For example:

> **Researcher:** Why did you read 'hose' there?
> **Reader:** 'Cos I sounded it out and that's what it says.
> **Researcher:** Does that make sense?
> **Reader:** (confused by question) I dunno.

I suppose that it could be argued that these readers **are** predicting but it is a very different sort of prediction. It seems to be based more on the 'wild guess' variety, stemming from an unsuccessful attempt to sound the letters out or to recall from rote memory a word which has a similar shape to the once causing the miscue.

5. Effective and ineffective readers use graphophonic knowledge differently.

When effective and ineffective readers are compared on the ways in which they use their knowledge of graphic/phonic correspondences, they show a striking difference. The effective reader uses his knowledge of letter shapes and sounds to confirm or reject his predictions, as did our reader who rejected 'bathers' for 'tea'. If one could get inside his head and be privy to his thoughts as he changed from 'bathers' to 'tea', one might have heard something like this:

> *I've predicted 'bathers' because that fits in semantically and it doesn't violate the grammatical structure of English (a plural noun can go there) but, wait a minute, when I look at the initial letter it's a 't', and what's more, it's only a small word. No, 'bathers' will never fit; I'd better back up, have a closer look at the graphics and see if there is an alternative which will fit in and which will also made sense and not violate the rules of English. I know! It's got to be 'tea'.*

Ineffective readers don't use their graphophonic knowledge in the same way because they don't predict in quite the same way. How can they? They have no storyline to help them. Instead, they use their knowledge of graphic and phonic relationships to try to unlock the pronunciation of the word. When one talks with them and tries to discover their reasons for doing this, two broad reasons emerge.

Some do it because they believe that this will enable them to get at the meaning of the text. Unfortunately, because this tactic is successful some of the time, those who use it are on the classic 'partial reinforcement schedule'. Like poker machine addicts, they get small reinforcements every now and then but eventually lose their stake — unless the text is specially designed to make this strategy work every time.

Others adopt the unlock-the-pronunciation strategy because they believe that this is what they're supposed to do. (I often wonder how they get to believe such things!)

6. Effective readers use a wider range of strategies.

When the ways in which effective readers go about dealing with difficult parts of any text are compared, they display knowledge of a wide range of strategies which they can and do bring to bear in order to help them over any form of 'reader's block'. Ineffective readers do not seem to have as many.

These kinds of data emerge when one actually observes readers in action, intervenes in the process and asks them to explain what they're doing when they appear to be 'blocked'.

This is what **effective readers** do when they're confronted with a blockage:

★ They pass over the blockage and try to pick up more clues to meaning, possibly coming back to the part which blocked them later.

★ They retreat to the beginning of the sentence in which the blockage occurs and, like a long-jumper who has 'fouled out', take another 'running jump' at the blockage, building up what might be called a 'head of linguistic steam', hoping that they'll get up enough momentum to help them across.

★ They leave out altogether that which is blocking them and skip over that piece of text, secure in knowledge that it is not going to affect the outcome of what it is they're reading.

★ They may try to sound if out if all else fails. 'Sounding out' usually consists of working out the sounds which the first couple of letters make. Typically, this is a last resort and is not as frequently done as the other strategies.

★ They ask someone — usually when they've finished reading reading the page on which the blockage occurs.

Ineffective readers do not employ as wide a range of strategies. My experience with many hundreds of such readers is that they have two basic strategies.

★ Sound it out. 'Sounding out' in this instance, usually means phonically attacking every letter or letter cluster in whatever is causing the blockage.

★ Look around helplessly, and hope someone will come to their aid and say the word which is causing the blockage.

It is also of interest to note that ineffective readers seem to fixate on difficult sections of text. They seem to be obsessed with getting something out. I've personally found it very difficult to get ineffective readers to go on, or to leave out the part that's blocking them. They seem to be prepared either to work at any blockage for inordinate periods of time or to give up at that point and not go beyond it if their attempts are unsuccessful. They are loathe to omit anything from the text.

7. Effective readers are more consciously aware of how they process print and of connections between various aspects of the processes.

Whenever I've intervened and asked both effective and ineffective readers about the ways they process print, I've been struck by how much more aware the more effective readers are about their own reading behaviour. I call this 'meta-textual' awareness. When asked to reflect upon what they do when they are blocked, they can bring to conscious awareness the processes which they actually use. Furthermore, some of the more mature readers are consciously aware of the relationships between processes. I can remember one avid, very advanced ten-year-old reader who informed me during an interview that she preferred reading fiction to non-fiction. When I probed and asked shy, she reflected for a few moments and replied,

"Well, I don't write non-fiction therefore I don't read it."

This reply suggests that she is consciously aware of the very subtle relationships which exist between reading and writing. Another ten-year-old from the same class, when asked how he'd learned to spell so well when he hadn't formally studied spelling as had the children in other classes, replied,

"I learned to spell by reading. When you're constantly reading and writing, you can't help learning to spell."

I would argue that this reply is indicative not only of an awareness of the subtle relationships which exist between reading, writing and spelling, but also of one's own learning processes.

Less effective, less mature readers do not typically display the same degrees of meta-textual awareness.

8. Effective readers are confident readers.

Effective readers ooze a quiet kind of confidence about the ability to deal with texts of all kinds. In some cases, it's almost arrogance! Melissa, the ten-year-old who didn't read much non-fiction because she didn't write it, informed me during an interview:

> "While there are books that I don't like to read, I've never yet found one that I can't read. I can read anything."

This confidence is reflected in many ways. It's closely related to a positive attitude toward books and a genuine love of reading. In a project which explored some of the characteristics of avid readers, Williams (1979) found that the most avid readers were also persistent readers who continued to persevere with difficult texts long after less avid readers had given up. Even when he presented them with texts which were highly specialised and esoteric and well beyond their background knowledge and language levels, avid readers continued to persevere with the task of trying to make meaning from them.

Ineffective readers are quite different. They lack confidence as readers. This lack manifests itself in different ways, ranging from avoidance behaviours, to attributing the fault to some rare complaint, to anxiety, to diet, etc. When one probes, one finds a common factor which ineffective readers share — the expectation that they will fail to understand the text.

The Fundamentals

Let's Go Forward to Them

At one time or another in our professional lives we've heard the catch cry, 'Back to basics!'. Although I value the notion of identifying what the basic principles of any situation are, I've never liked the notion of regressing. Nor have I been enamoured with the nature of the basics which are often held up as the panacea of reading pedagogy. Too often I've found that they're basics which are not grounded in real reading behaviour at all. I much prefer a slogan which Professor Michael Halliday presented at a conference some years ago, namely 'Forward to the Fundamentals'.

I want to argue that if we could synthesise what we know about effective readers into a series of short, precise points, we might produce a set of principles which are fundamental for effective reading to occur. Here is my attempt to draw up such a set of fundamentals.

Fundamentals which Should Be Taught to Learner Readers

1. **Sensible coherent meaning should be the end result of reading.**
   Alternative form: Semantic and syntactic nonsense should never be tolerated.

2. **Effective reading necessitates being able to use semantic, syntactic and graphic information in mutually supportive ways.**
   Alternative form: There is more than one form of information that readers must learn to use.

3. **Effective reading necessitates being able to predict on the basis of syntactic and semantic information.**
   Alternative form: There's more to reading than word recognition based on graphophonic knowledge.

4. **Effective reading necessitates being able to confirm and/ or reject predictions, often using graphophonic knowledge.**
   Alternative form: Graphophonic analysis is most useful when used in conjunction with effective prediction.

5. **Effective reading necessitates the use of a wide range of processing strategies when dealing with reader's block.**
   Alternative form: There's more to reading than being able to sound out unknown words.

6. **Effective reading is promoted by conscious awareness of the processes involved.**
   Alternative form: Good readers know how they do it.

7. **Effective readers are confident, positive readers.**
   Alternative form: Most learner readers expect to be able to read anything. They generally believe this until told by someone that it isn't true.

I would argue that these fundamentals are really the aims and objectives which teachers of all grade levels, K—12, should be aspiring to achieve with respect to their reading programmes. The kindergarten teacher and the high school science teacher should be trying to achieve the same things with their pupils. The only variance would be the complexity of the material which they would use as the medium through which these aims/objectives were achieved. I would also argue that the principles of natural learning which I've detailed in

Chapters 4, 5 and 6 also apply to these fundamentals. Learner readers need to be **immersed** in the kinds of texts we think are appropriate for their current needs. They need repeated **demonstrations** of how to read, how to overcome blockages, and how to **make explicit** and reflect upon what they have both learned to do and still need to learn to do. These demonstrations can be either in the form of artifacts (good texts to read and learn from) or actions (thinking aloud as reading is done, reading/thinking orally, etc.). They need to be given **responsibility** for choosing what they read. They need to be given **expectations** that they will read certain materials and that they can read anything if they want to. They must be allowed to **approximate** meanings. They must be given time to **engage** in the reading act and to **employ** and thus modify and extend their reading prowess. They must be able to receive both support and **feedback** as they struggle to construct meaning from print.

In short, there are no reasons why learning to read or getting to be a more mature reader, cannot follow the same principles which underlie learning to talk or getting to be a more mature talker. All that needs to be done is to marry what Chapter 8 says about reading with what Chapter 4 says about learning.

9

Making Connections II: Understanding Writing

In the previous chapter I outlined what I believe teachers need to know and understand about reading in order to teach it from a holistic perspective. I emphasised the necessity for connecting this information to the model of learning which had been described in earlier chapters.

In this chapter I intend to do much the same kind of thing with respect to writing. I am going to explore the same questions:

  (1) **What is writing?**
  (2) **How does writing happen?**
  (3) **What have effective writers learned to do?**

It will become obvious that I have found it very difficult to separate reading and writing, except at a superficial level. As I drafted and revised this chapter I became aware of how similar these forms of language behaviour really are. This difficulty served to reinforce for me the parallel nature of most forms of language. It also reinforced the notion that languages and different forms of language are really defined by their interconnections. What gives any particular element of language its particular role in that language has little to do with its superficial physical properties. Rather, it is the relationships it enters into with other elements, forms or systems of language which are crucial. Thus, the phonemic system, the syntactic system, the semantic system, the graphic system and so on, are all interconnected. There are certain conventions about how these connections should be made that writers must learn to apply if what they set out to write is going to achieve its aim. These conventions go far beyond superficial things like spelling and punctuation. They extend also to the deeper aspects of language organisation such as the structure which is associated with certain kinds of writing. A narrative has a certain kind of organisation which is different from a report which is, in turn, different from a persuasive argument, and so on and so on. These different organisations are partly a function of the patterns of phonemic, semantic and syntactic interconnections which the author needs to make if the text is to have its conventional, expected shape.

At another level, reading as a form of language behaviour is connected to writing, which is connected to listening and speaking and sign language and so on.

In knowing or learning about how one element, form or system connects with others, one comes to learn and know about the system in toto.

Not only are languages and language forms defined by their interconnections, but they are learned when these interconnections are realised by the learner.

All of this merely serves to reinforce the conceptual validity and usefulness of the notion that language learners need to have multiple reading, writing, speaking and listening encounters so that these forms of language can all feed into a central linguistic data pool where the interconnections can be worked out and stored.

What Is Writing?

Like reading, writing is a form of language behaviour which involves both **construction** and **comprehension** of a text. Writers construct texts for potential readers to comprehend. In order to do this, writers, like readers, need to bring to bear certain kinds of knowledge, skills and procedures. Although there are some differences, the kind of knowledge, skills and procedures overlap considerably. For example, like readers, writers need to have a highly developed sense of comprehension. Writers need to comprehend not only their messages (how else can they construct them?) but they need also to comprehend the reasons or purposes for constructing them, the audiences who they wish to read them, and so on. Like readers, in order to achieve their ends they need to have certain semantic, syntactic, graphophonic and other kinds of language knowledge available and ready to be put into practice.

On the surface it looks like writing exists merely to serve the purposes of communication and I suppose in one sense this is true. However, it should also be kept in mind that one potential reader of a piece of any writing is the author of that piece himself. In fact, no writer can avoid reading the text which is being constructed. (I have lost count of the number of times that I have read this text, both as I compose it and after it's been composed.) This form of communication, referred to by Moffett as "communication within the same nervous system" (**Moffett, 1968**), is a special kind of communication which serves a deeper, more cognitive and affective set of purposes than the mere transmission of information. And this is where the important difference lies between writing as a form of language behaviour, and reading.

Readers can read without necessarily being writers or knowing a great deal about writing and how it's done. But writers must be readers, and this creates a kind of language and thinking behaviour which is quite unique.

When writers read their own writing, not only do they communicate meanings to themselves, but they discover how to order their thinking and their worlds. The act of writing, of trying to construct a text and then re-reading that text, seems to bring to conscious awareness ideas, concepts, themes, and ways of organising thoughts, messages and meanings, which were previously unknown to the writer-reader at the conscious level. This process of constantly re-reading one's own text also has far-reaching effects on the way one reads, and ultimately on the range of different textual forms that one comes to control.

Thus, while communication with others is certainly one of the primary purposes for engaging in writing, it is not necessarily **the** major reason for it. Writing also serves the function of helping us to organise and understand our lives and our worlds. It is probably the most powerful, readily available form of extending thinking and learning that the human race has available to it. There is no other technology that has quite the same potential for ordering and developing human thinking. Cultures which have discovered writing are very different from those which have not. It must be a useful development for, as Smith notes, no culture which has developed writing has ever subsequently given it up. *(Smith, 1982)*

Prolonged engagement with writing seems to affect ways of thinking. Jaynes, in his monumental; work on the origins of consciousness in the human race *(Jaynes, 1976)* goes as far as asserting that the discovery of writing was instrumental in the development of conscious thought as we know it today. Scollan, in his work with Alaskan native people, has drawn attention to the subtle ways in which the traditional ways of thinking and interacting are being affected by the influence of the imposition of a written language on a previously non-literate people. *(Scollan, 1987)* The evidence, to my mind, is quite conclusive:

Sustained engagement with writing also means sustained engagement with reading. Both result in sustained engagement with written text which does something to the way we think, interact, learn and use language. It causes the internalisation of different forms of language and different modes of thinking. While some cultures may not value what it does to ways of thinking, e.g. the elders of the Alaskan people Scollan has been studying, our culture does.

It is my belief that when we set out to teach writing, its role as:

    a) a medium for extending and developing thought,
    b) a means of ordering and creating worlds,
    c) a mechanism for bringing to conscious awareness that which was previously unconscious,
    d) a method for developing the language skills which both empower and dignify,

should be kept clearly to the fore.

How Does Writing Happen?

When this question was raised with respect to reading, it helped us to focus on the cognitive processes which were involved. We used the conceptual framework of miscue analysis to peel away the layers of assumption and guesswork which surrounded the miracle we call reading. In a metaphorical sense we got inside the reader's head and reconstructed the processes that take place when reading happens. I argued that this kind of knowledge would help teachers teacher reading more effectively.

I've found it extremely difficult to do the same thing with respect to writing for two reasons:

Firstly, most of what happens during the activity of writing occurs at a subconscious level and is therefore invisible to an observer. I realise that in this sense writing is no different from silent reading behaviour. However, what one reads silently one can also read aloud, and given a framework like miscue analysis, it is possible to 'open a window' on the mind and gain some insights into how reading happens. I know of no framework analogous to miscue analysis which can be applied to writing. Of course, it is possible to observe writers in action and document their overt behaviours, and this form of research into the writing process has been extremely valuable in providing some insights into it. But these observations can only take theory building so far. In order to understand how writing happens, researchers need to find ways of tapping into the subconscious, covert aspects of writing. To date, researchers seem to have been restricted to a relatively small range of procedures for doing this, including:

— unstructured, probing interviews with both immature and mature writers as they are composing and transcribing;
— retrospective and introspective musings of established writers;
— introspective analyses by writing researchers.

In other words, given the current state of research technology, what we find out about writing has to be inferred from observable behaviour and from what learners and writers tell us about what they think happens when they write.

Secondly, it is quite artificial to try to deal with reading and writing either as if they are separate domains of concern (as most teachers do when they timetable writing and reading separately), or as if they are related by being mirror images of each other (writing being the productive form of language; reading the receptive). Rather, reading and writing have a relationship which is of a different order. It is this:

Writing encapsulates reading.

As previously noted, while reading can happen in the absence of highly developed knowledge of or skill in writing, writing cannot happen in the absence of reading. The reading which occurs in association with writing is of two kinds. Firstly, there is the reading and re-reading of the written text as it is being constructed, or **reading which accompanies the written text**. Secondly, there is the sum total of all the reading that the writer has carried out prior to writing the actual text. Whenever writers sit before a blank page and begin to write, they call upon the knowledge that the reading of other texts has stored in their linguistic data pools. This is **reading which precedes the writing of a text**.

Both kinds of reading are inextricably bound up with the act of writing. Any theory of how writing happens must include a theory of how reading happens as well. What one ends up with is a theory of how written texts are constructed.

Okay — So, How are Written Texts Constructed?

My research base for answering this question is no different from those listed previously. If I add my own introspections about my own writing behaviour to some of the data I have collected from learner writers I have observed and interviewed, I come up with the following explanatory account.

First, the 'Whole Picture'

The writing act is made up of two broad categories — dare I call them behaviours? — namely, **subconscious components** and **observable components.**

There are three major subconscious, and therefore covert, components, namely:

> **Intention**
> **Decision-making**
> **Selection**

There are three major observable, and therefore overt, components, namely:

> **Reading**
> **Writing down**
> **Talking**

These two sets of components support, interact and influence each other in ways that we don't yet fully understand.

The Subconscious Components

Intention

Every written text begins with the development of an **intention** in the writer. In the first instance, this intention is typically global and non-specific. The potential writer, for some reason, feels the need to create a written text of some sort. The reason could be as mundane as writing a reminder note to oneself about an appointment which must be kept, or a shopping list, or it may be as esoteric and/or complex as a poem to one's lover, a letter complaining to the council about the garbage collection, a thesis for a doctorate, or the Great Australian Novel. It could be an intention that is precipitated by another agent, such as a teacher who asks for a story or a report. The level of specificity of intent is variable but in most instances it is at the whole task level, i.e. the intent is to write the letter about the rough treatment that the garbage collector gives your bin, or to write the novel about the experiences of being a teenager in the slums, or to write a report about lemmings. Few of the specific details of the precise form it will eventually have, or of the specific content it might include, or of the actual words which will be used, are clearly known at this time, although as deadlines for the text become closer some of these more molecular specifications — sub-headings, arguments, specific topics — will begin to emerge.

Decision-making

The realisation of intent in consciousness precipitates a series of decisions. The retrospective recounts, introspections and interview data from established writers and writer-researchers indicate that these decisions typically revolve around questions of:

> **Purpose** Why am I writing this? What do I want to achieve?
> **Audience** Who is it for? What is to be my relationship with my audience?
> **Information** What information do I have? What do I need?
> **Content** What is the text going to be about? What is my focus?
> **Procedure** What will I use — pen or pencil? Where will I start? What will I do first?

Ineffective and/or immature writers must also make decisions but often they are of a different order from those which effective writers say they make. I used to think that this was a developmental matter. However, some recent research by one of my colleagues has shown that very young writers can and do ask the same kinds of sophisticated questions and attempt to make the same kinds of decisions about purpose, audience, process and information as do effective users of writing. All they need are appropriate models to be demonstrated and the thinking behind these models to be made explicit for them. They also need to have been convinced that writing is a worthwhile activity which they are capable of learning to control. *(Turbill, 1987)* This is another way of stating that, given the appropriate context and conditions, learner writers can be helped to use the same processes that effective writers use.

Of course, we've all met learner writers who seem to persist in investing most of their cognitive energy resolving decisions associated with surface, textual features such as spelling, punctuation and handwriting, paying little attention to purpose, audience, information and content. Why they do this is not really hard to understand. The theory which lies at the core of this book would argue strongly that it's been caused by a combination of how or what they've been taught, and what they already know.

Selection

The way in which decisions about purpose, audience, information, contact and process are resolved, precipitates **selection** behaviour. Writers must choose from their range of linguistic options the most appropriate sounds, words and ways of organising those words, to achieve their intent. Every writer has a repertoire of linguistic knowledge which can be used in order to complete the writing task. From the perspective of selection, constructing the written text entails the following:

Selecting, from the options which are in the linguistic data pool, forms of words and ways of organising these which will best solve the writing problem which the intent and decision-making has created. In most instances, this is an unconscious process which occurs, on some occasions, in time sequences that can only be measured in microseconds, while on other occasions it can take significantly longer. (I've been trying to construct this chapter for several weeks now!)

It is important to realise that the form which any written text ultimately takes is a consequence of these linguistic choices. It is also important to realise that the so-called 'success' of any piece of text depends on which options the writer has used.

An Elaboration of the Notion of Selection

Let us examine in more detail what the notion of "selection of linguistic options" means, by looking at an example of two texts written by the same Grade 5 child. Peter wrote both these texts within a month of each other. Both grew out of an 'arctic animals' theme which his class had been studying.

Text #1: A Report

LEMMINGS

Lemmings are small furry animals that look like hamsters. They live in the arctic. Lemmings do not hibernate or turn white in winter. A female lemming can produce eight litters of five or six a year. Because of its rapid reproduction most animals are not getting enough food, so they have to move across the tundra. Most lemmings are eaten by snowy owls, arctic foxes or wolves, and many die crossing the rivers. When summer comes lemmings store food in their burrows to eat in winter. When winter comes lemmings are safe underground and are well fed with grasses and other plants. If a lemming should decide to come out it will freeze very quickly, unless a predator spots it first.

Text #2: A Narrative

THE TALE OF LEPPY THE LEMMING

Far, far away in the arctic circle in a small burrow under the snow lived Leppy the lemming. Winter was nearly over and Leppy, his five sisters, and his mother were waiting for the first signs of spring so that they could leave their burrow and begin eating the fresh spring grass which would soon be on the tundra. It was time for them to leave the safety of their burrow and move out on their own to begin their families.

At last the day came. But alas, as Mother lemming cautiously left the burrow, sniffing the air cautiously a large arctic owl swooped down and almost caught her and carried her off. She rushed back down the burrow and told Leppy and his sisters that they could not leave just yet as it was too dangerous. They were trapped, and would soon starve unless they could get out and feed on the fresh spring grass. They had to work out a way to escape the clutches of the owl.

Leppy had an idea. He took his mother's sewing kit and one of her old dresses and sewed and sewed all night. In the morning he had made a look-alike lemming by stuffing the clothes he had sewn with some of the grass and roots their mother had stored from her collecting and gathering last summer. At first light they threw it out on to the space at the front of their burrow. The owl swooped and was away with the dummy before you could give two hoots. Before it realised that it had been tricked Leppy and his family were free and safe, ready to feed on the summer pastures. Leppy and his family lived happily ever after.

Peter's first text displays many of the organisational criteria and linguistic forms which identify the textual form known as 'report'. According to Martin & Rothery (1980) a report has the following features:

★ It deals with factual information.
★ It focuses on a group or class of things rather than an individual.
★ It may describe an experience or report on the information that has been gathered.

★ It has a general introduction to the thing to be talked about which is followed by descriptions of specific aspects of the subject.
★ It may contain generalisations, classifications and/or explanations.
★ The writer does not make any personal comment.

On the other hand, Peter's second text displays many of the organisational criteria and linguistic forms which are characteristic of the textual form known as the narrative. According to Martin & Rothery a narrative has the following features:

★ **An orientation** — sets the scene and introduces the main characters.
★ **A complication** — something happens.
★ **A resolution** — the complication is resolved. (A number of different complications and resolutions may occur in the one narrative.)
★ **A coda** — a comment on the story as a whole may be tacked onto the end.

Peter's decision to write both a report and a narrative about the same domain of concern involved him in some very nimble linguistic footwork. In the process of writing each piece he had to delve within his linguistic data pool to find at least two kinds of data:
— data which related to the organisation of each piece;
— data pertaining to the sounds, words and syntactic options he had available which would best support this organisation.

His choice of words for each piece intuitively seems to be appropriate. It seems appropriate that a narrative, or story as it is typically called, should begin with words such as 'Far, far away . . .' and make use of such constructions as '. . . lived Leppy the lemming'. We expect it to contain phrases like 'It was time for . . .', 'At last the day came . . .', 'At first light . . .', 'But alas . . .' and '. . . sewed and sewed . . .' We expect it to be in the past tense. We expect it to entertain or amuse. It seems to fulfil most of the conventions we have come to associate with a narrative text.

On the other hand, his report uses quite different sorts of words which again seem to be appropriate. We expect reports to contain words like 'hibernate' rather than sleep, 'female lemming' rather than mother lemming, 'litter' rather than five sisters or family. We expect reports to use the present tense. We expect them to begin with statements which introduce the topic, rather than the setting. We expect reports to flesh out the details of whatever the topic is. We expect reports to inform and explain. In order to do this, Peter had to make linguistic choices which met these expectations. He needed to be either intuitively or consciously aware of the following:

a) that language used to amuse or entertain is different from language used to explain.
b) that these differences are compounded by the relationship one has with the intended audience. For example, the language one uses to entertain or inform a close relative or acquaintance is different from that which one uses to entertain and/or inform an audience at a conference of academic peers whom one has never met.
c) that all of these, and many other, variables will affect the way that he realises his intended meanings.

In order to meet these expectations, Peter needed to choose from the range of linguistic options he carried around inside his head. When I interviewed him about these two pieces he informed me that in each piece the female lemming was, in his mind, the same one, and that the litter of five or six in the report was really Leppy and his five sisters in the narrative. In other words, because of the decisions he made about purpose and audience, etc., he had been constrained to use different sets of words to refer to what were essentially, in his mind at least, the same objects.

If his texts are to be successful, he really can't do anything else. While *Scintillate, scintillate, diminutive asteroid, I often speculate as to your existential status* has some of the characteristics of the famous nursery rhyme, it doesn't sound quite as right as *Twinkle, twinkle, little star, how I wonder what you are.* Similarly, it would sound quite inappropriate for Peter to begin his report with 'Far, far away in the arctic circle . . .' If he did, the meanings he intended would not be realised.

The question is, of course, how do learner writers like Peter get inside their heads all the knowledge of language and language forms which enable them to make the appropriate linguistic choices? The simple answer is that they must engage with demonstrations of them. They must read and/or hear other texts which demonstrate these features and then take the decision to engage with them.

The Observable Components

Reading, Writing Down, Talking

The subconscious, and therefore invisible, components of writing behaviour which I've described above, are accompanied by overt behaviours which seem to work both in tandem with, and as a consequence of, those which are subconscious. They also interact with each other. The most common forms of these overt behaviours are **reading**, **writing down** and **talking**.

Here's what I think happens. The subconscious **intentions, decisions** and **linguistic choices** are made manifest through either **talking** behaviour (to oneself or to another or both) or **writing down** behaviour, or both. Each of these overt behaviours is usually accompanied by **reading**. The writer reads what he/she has written and reflects on what is there. In other words, the writer reconsiders the subconscious intent, decision and choices which had been made previously, perhaps only a few milliseconds ago. This reading and/or talking typically leads to changes, especially in the early states of writing a piece. These can be changes of intent, changes of previously-made decisions, changes in a previously chosen linguistic option, or changes in all three. On some occasions the reading behaviour will change slightly. As well as reading and re-reading the text which is being constructed, writers will read what other authors have written, and then turn back to their own writing again, possibly changing words and phrases in the developing text. These changes set the cycle going again. And again. And again and again. More writing down, more reading, more talking, more reflecting . . . followed by more changes in intent, different decisions, a new set of linguistic options, and so on. Ultimately, it leads to fewer and fewer changes until the writer decides that the piece is finished.[1] This is what is traditionally called drafting, revising, rewriting, etc. but it doesn't occur in any kind of simple, linear or recipe form. Rather, it's a process of constantly putting a set of linguistic plans on paper and then constantly changing them as the talking, reading and writing down proceeds.

What becomes obvious is that it is almost impossible to discuss sensibly questions such as "What happens in writing?" using simple categories like 'composing' and 'writing down' or by developing the kind of simple, linear, descriptive schema which have become popular in the last few years. While it might be conceptually cleaner and organisationally simpler to divide the period of time between the original intention to write and a finished written product into phases like 'pre-writing', 'writing' and 'rewriting', such schema run the risk of creating a static stages metaphor which can be quite misleading. In reality, writing involves a constant and unpredictable movement between a wide range of behaviours. As Robert Protherough states:

> ". . . people do not follow any one set of activities but shuffle to and fro between initiating ideas, relating items, writing, revising and proofreading." **(Protherough, 1983, p.146)**

---

[1] The word 'finished' is in quotation marks because some writers never believe their pieces are finished. There is a popular story about how Tolstoy used to begin rewriting his published pieces if ever he came across them in a magazine.

What Have Effective Writers Learned to Do?

In the previous chapter I argued that teachers would be better equipped to teach reading if they had some idea of where they should be heading. By this I meant that if teachers had some idea of what 'good' reading was and what 'good' readers did, they would be in a better position to make decisions about how they should go about teaching immature or underdeveloped readers.

I hold the same views with respect to writing, but when I tried to do the same thing I found it a more complex exercise. The complexity is associated with the nature of literary taste.

How do we recognise 'good' writing when we come across it? How can we recognise a 'good' writer when we come across one? These are difficult questions to answer in ways which teachers find useful because the questions presuppose that someone, somewhere, has worked out what 'good' writing actually is, and can describe it in terms of a universally agreed upon set of characteristics. This is, of course, impossible without resorting to subjective values. No one, to my knowledge, has so far been able to devise a set of context-free, objective, value-free criteria for defining 'good' writing or describing what it looks like. The reason for this difficulty is quite simple.

Like reading, writing is about the creation of meaning. How does one judge the quality of a piece of meaning?

The work of linguists, sociolinguists, literary critics, rhetoricians and others has shown that the meaning of any piece of written text is a function of a host of interacting contextual factors: purpose, audience, topic, print layout and orientation, reader's background experience and values, and so on. Pinning down and defining something as conceptually slippery as quality of meaning is simply too difficult given the current state of linguistic science.

I've found it much more useful and helpful to renegotiate the question. Instead of "What is good writing?" or "What is an effective writer?" I find it easier to ask:

What characterises an effective user of writing?

In order to answer this question, I've drawn on a number of sources of data, including:

- regular and systematic observations I've made of learner writers,
- statements made by successful authors of both fiction and non-fiction,
- statements made by writer researchers,

- introspective observations of myself as an author — admittedly, one who writes a certain kind of prose for a particular kind of audience,
- regular and systematic observations and interviews with ineffective users of writing — namely, those university students who come to my centre for help with writing.

When I pull the threads from all of these sources of data together, the following profile of an effective user of writing emerges.

An effective user of writing is:

1. A confident user of the medium.

The effective writers whom I've observed have no hang-ups or qualms about using writing to meet a whole range of needs.

Implications for teaching: Learner writers must be treated in ways which convince them that writing is learnable by them. This means conveying the appropriate expectations about writing.

2. A person who feels positive about writing, or at least is not alienated from getting involved in it.

What is interesting is that there is plenty of evidence which indicates that very young children who are just setting out on the path to literacy do actually behave toward writing and the creation of meaning using writing in very positive ways. It is only as they go through school that these attitudes seem to change.

Implications for teaching: Learner writers need to be treated in ways that convince them that writing is not only learnable but that it is really an exciting, interesting and satisfying enterprise which will further the purposes of their lives.

3. One who is committed to one's own writing.

Such commitment manifests itself in two ways: as both a strong sense of ownership for one's own meanings, as well as a strong sensitivity towards the ways in which readers will react to them. This is a double-edged sword, a finely balanced condition. The effective users of writing I've observed and interviewed can make decisions about meaning and form, and can also choose from the options which are available to them. At the same time they not only show a continually developing ability to judge and evaluate the effect that their written texts have on audiences but they become more willing and ready to accept advice and/or revise their words because of the responses which others might make.

Implications for teaching: Learner writers need to be able to make decisions and choose from several options. They must also be ready to justify their options, particularly those relating to the words and phrases they choose when creating texts. They must share their work, often with listeners whom they trust. This means creating a community of caring and sensitive authors. Teachers frequently need to model being a caring and sensitive co-author.

4. **A person who can talk about and make explicit what he knows about writing.**

Effective users of writing display increasing degrees of understanding of the ways that writing can be used, of the different purposes for writing, and of the processes which are involved in using writing for these different purposes. I call this 'meta-textual awareness' and will refer to it in more detail later in the chapter. In our research we have been continually surprised by the levels of meta-textual awareness which even very young writers can develop.

Implications for teaching: Teachers need to model, by thinking out loud, the processes and knowledge which they use when they create texts. For example, they need to model how all effective users of writing resolve the decisions about purpose, audience, information, content and process. As well, they must continually model or draw their learners' attention to the salient bits of any demonstration and/or model. They should never try to simplify or fragment this knowledge or these processes.

5. **One who demonstrates increasing degrees of control over different textual forms.**

I have found it useful to define, operationally, "control of a textual form" as the ability to read and write exemplars of that form independently. Thus when Chelsea's reading log (Grade 5) showed that she had read and discussed in class ten fables, and written three of her own which were similar to the one reproduced below, I felt safe in claiming that she had developed control of the textual form we have labelled the fable.

SLY OLD FOX by Chelsea Capetta

Once there was a sly old fox who loved plump juicy chickens for his meals. One morning he found a large opening in the chicken wire on a farmer's farm. It was a bit right for very hungry foxes, so he crept inside, took a plump chicken and ran away to eat it. Next day the fox jumped through the wire and grabbed a chicken and hurried away. This went on for days and days. All of a sudden, no more chickens. Then the fox grew thin and died and that taught him a lesson. **Moral:** Take all, Lose all.

Similarly, when the reading log of one of Chelsea's classmates, Peter, showed that he had read and discussed a number of books and articles which reported factual material, and that he had written several pieces which we classified as 'reports' similar to the one reproduced previously about lemmings, I felt safe in claiming that Peter had demonstrated control of the textual form we called 'the report'. My data show that under appropriate conditions (such as those described in Mrs Brown's class, Chapter 7), learner writers display more and more control over a wider and wider variety of textual forms.

Implications for teaching: If they are to make appropriate linguistic choices, learners must be continually filling their linguistic data pools. Sustained immersion in different textual forms, demonstrations of how they are written, models of finished products, conscious awareness of how different texts are structured, time to engage in realistic tasks of using and constructing such textual forms, are all necessary strategies.

Meta-textual Awareness?

What has this to do with learning to be literate?

In my research with literacy learners I've found a very strong relationship consistently emerging. It is this: those whom I've considered to be the most effective users of reading and writing are also those who can tell me the most about the processes and knowledge they use in order to read and write. They display high levels of what I have previously referred to as 'meta-textual awareness', that is, conscious awareness of how they read and write, how they deal with reading and writing problems, how they learn, and so on.

My data are replete with examples of this kind of knowledge. Although this excerpt from eight-year-old Matthew's interview deals specifically with writing, it is an example of what I mean.

> **BC:** Tell me about writing. Do you like writing?
> **MR:** Yes! I love making up fictional stories. Mostly I get my ideas from fictional books. They give me ideas for future stories. They give me really good ideas. If you want to make a really good emotional story you should read books with emotion in them. If you want to write a good, non-fiction piece you should read a non-fiction book.

These statements indicate that Matthew has made some very subtle connections between reading, writing and his own learning. When I analysed all those data which related to this notion of meta-textual awareness I found a certain pattern emerging: the meta-textual awarenesses which the more effective users of reading and writing had, was essentially a web of knowledge which helped them make certain kinds of connections or links. These connections were of three kinds:

(i) Connections between processes

Like Matthew, most effective users of writing with whom I've been working could talk about and explain how learning and reading and writing were connected. For example, they could talk about how they learned to spell and punctuate through the acts of reading and writing, or how and where they got their ideas and models for writing, or how talking things through with others helped them solve reading/writing problems, and so on.

(ii) Connections within processes

I described in an earlier chapter how effective readers could talk about the differences between skim reading and reading for other purposes. Effective writers can do much the same thing with respect to writing. In my data, for example, learner writers talk knowledgeably about leads and endings; the powers of details in writing; how one drafts or when one edits; why conventions are important in public drafts; what they do when they're blocked, and so on.

(iii) Connections between texts

Effective learners whom I interviewed could also talk about the similarities between the plot, settings, characters and techniques which they used in their own writing. They could relate this information to the ways that authors whose work they read created plot, setting, effect and so on. Here are some direct quotes from some of the interview data I've analysed:

"The fairy tales I've written are different from my fables in the following ways . . . "

"I'm writing a kind of fairy tale which has a moral like a fable does, but you have to work it out — I won't actually say it."

"You know how the characters in 'The Twits' appear in 'Boy' with different names? Well, I've done something like that in this piece . . ."

"I've used similes like Colin Thiele does."

"I've tried to do what E. B. White does when he describes how lonely Wilbur was."

"I've tried to make word pictures like Roald Dahl does in some of his books . . . "

They could also, in rather fumbling ways, explain how they thought fiction differed from non-fiction, how report differed from story, how argument differed from description, and so on.

Why does this kind of conscious awareness about texts and language and learning and reading and writing appear to enhance the degrees of control which learners seem to develop?

I believe that it's got something to do with what Gregory Bateson referred to as "the pattern which connects". *(Bateson, 1979)* His argument is that quality learning is contingent upon the learner being able to work out the patterns which connect. His thesis is that real learning (quality learning) is primarily about making the connections which illuminate what I have called "the big picture". *(Cambourne, 1987)* This is what these learners appear to be doing with respect to writing and authorcraft (and language, and learning, and reading, etc.).

What is interesting is that they know how they learned to make these connections: (a) by attending to their teacher's demonstrations of the connections she made as she thought out loud, or made explicit what she knew and did when she wrote and read, and (b) by talking writing-related problems through with their peers and their teacher.

The Basics of Writing

The characteristics of effective users of writing can be used to make explicit what the basics of a writing curriculum ought to be. Furthermore, I would argue that such basics would be appropriate to all grade levels.

1. A strong conviction that writing is a worthwhile enterprise.

Learning to write is a complex enterprise. Learner writers need to be convinced that learning to write is worthwhile and will further the purposes of their lives, immeasurably enriching them. Ineffective users of writing are usually reluctant writers who avoid engaging in acts of writing if at all possible.

2. Knowledge of how writing can be used.

Effective users of writing know of, and appreciate, the power of writing as a means of learning, modifying and creating thought, extending ideas, and coping with emotional issues. They don't regard writing only as a medium for communicating with others.

3. Confidence.

Effective writers are confident writers. They are confident about their ability to use writing for both communicative and thinking-learning tasks. Ineffective writers lack confidence and are very teacher-dependent.

4. Readiness to use writing.

There seems to be little point in teaching learners to write if, after having learned, they use writing reluctantly. Effective writers turn readily to writing when they need to communicate, or to solve both conceptual and affective problems, or to think their way through a learning task.

5. Meta-textual awareness.

Learner writers should know at the conscious level how they write, what processes are involved and what strategies are available for them to use to help with their writing tasks. My research has convinced me that there is a connection between the level of meta-textual awareness and the effectiveness of a writer. Just what the precise nature of this relationship is, I am not certain. Is one an effective user of writing because one can make increasingly more explicit what I have called the subconscious processes of writing, or does one become more meta-textually aware because one is an effective user of writing? Whatever the precise form of the connection, one of the basics of my writing curriculum would be the development of the learner writer's conscious awareness of the subconscious processes and knowledge involved in writing, including:

— how the decisions about purpose, audience, knowledge, information and procedure can affect the form that any piece of writing will take;
— how writing, reading, talking and learning are connected and can be used to support each other;
— how different textual forms are organised;
— the processes that other writers have found effective for helping them complete their writing tasks,
— the questions which writers can ask when drafting a piece of writing.

6. An ever-increasing familiarity with different textual forms.

Sustained engagement with written text does something to the way that one thinks and solves problems. *Regular and sustained use of writing leads to high degrees of control over language, as does familiarity with a wide range of textual forms. Increased language control leads to intellectual, social and economic empowerment.* Our society values and rewards those who have this power.

Of course, not everybody thinks this way. The empowerment coming through the control of language and thinking which writing makes possible is threatening to some levels of society. The writer who knows how to use writing to develop his mind and clarify his thinking is a potentially dangerous individual — especially is he decides to write out his thoughts and theories in order to influence other people or perhaps change the status quo. Many of the political and social revolutions which have occurred throughout recent history have been influenced by writers who not only know **how** to use writing, but went ahead and used it. The old aphorism about the pen being mightier than the sword is an extension of this notion of empowerment through control of linguistic forms. Perhaps this lies at the root of some conservative views about how writing should be taught?

The principles which I've argued underpin learning to talk and read also apply to learning to write. In fact, if one substituted 'learner writer' for 'learner reader' and 'write' or 'writing' for 'read' or 'reading', the concluding paragraphs of the previous chapter could have been used here without any serious loss of meaning.

10

Pulling the Threads Together

What kind of literacy do we want for our nation as we enter the 21st century? This is an important question which politicians, employers, educators, and the community in general, must answer. Should the schools aim to increase the rates of so-called "functional literacy" ("enough to get by on", *Boomer, 1987*), or should they be aiming to produce graduates who demonstrate a **critical, active, productive literacy** *(Boomer)*. The answer to this question is basically ideological and ultimately will be resolved politically.

My ideological preferences should, by now, be obvious. As a nation, I believe that we need more than mere functional literacy if we are going to survive economically, socially and intellectually in the 21st century. We need school graduates who have access to, and who can control, those written language forms which make higher level thinking and knowing possible. My research over the last decade has convinced me that most of the so-called "traditional" or "back to basics" teaching is not really based on the aim of increasing the levels of literacy. Rather, these approaches are aimed at increasing the number of graduates who are functionally literate. Of course, the advocates of these approaches would argue that they **are** concerned with the same kind of literacy that I'm advocating. Probably, deep down, they are sincerely convinced of this.

Unfortunately, they are prisoners of a view of learning which makes the achievement of higher levels of literacy virtually impossible for the majority of our school children. The model of learning which drives so-called traditional, back-to-basics approaches to literacy is one which, in the long run, produces what I have referred to elsewhere as "dependent, a-literate" learners. These are "learners who can read and write (at least, according to their scores on standardised tests they can), but who prefer not to, and who need to be continually told what to do when confronted with learning tasks" *(Cambourne, 1987).*

The Principles of Whole Language

The thesis at the core of this book is that powerful, critical, active, productive literacy can be achieved systematically, regularly and relatively painlessly, with larger numbers of the school population, if certain learning principles are understood and practised. If the kind of literacy that Boomer and others are advocating is to become a reality, then learners need:

a) **immersion** in appropriate texts.
b) appropriate **demonstrations**.
c) the **responsibility** for making some decisions about when, how and what they read and write.
d) high **expectations** about themselves as potential readers and writers.
e) high **expectations** about their abilities to complete the reading and writing tasks they attempt.
f) freedom to **approximate** mature and/or 'ideal' forms of reading and writing.
g) time to **engage** in the acts of reading and writing.
h) opportunities to **employ** developing reading and writing skills and knowledge, in meaningful and purposeful contexts.
i) **responses** and feedback from knowledgeable others which both support and inform their attempts at constructing meaning using written language.
j) plenty of **opportunities**, with respect to the written form of language, to reflect upon and make explicit what they are learning.

These principles are not new. They constitute the core of a movement in literacy education which has been around in various guises for a long time but which has started to gather momentum over the last decade. Currently, it conforms to what is known as a whole language approach.

The nub of this approach lies in the nature of the demonstrations to which learners are exposed. Essentially, the argument is that in order to maximise learning, teachers should base their teaching of literacy on demonstrations of wholes of language rather than fragments. This is how I would define what I mean by whole language:

In a teaching-learning context, a whole language approach means that the literacy act or artifact being demonstrated needs to be sufficiently 'whole' to provide enough information about the various systems and sub-systems of language, so that learners, if they decide to engage, will have the data available for working out how all the pieces fit together and interact with each other.

The notion of 'wholeness', as I see it applying to whole language, is linked to the demonstrations with which the learner is expected to engage.

So what? Is that all this book is? Just another book about method?

Nothing could be further from the truth. Implicit in this way of defining whole language is a theory of learning second forms of language, be they written forms of an already acquired language, or new languages altogether, or any oral or written registers of a language. It is a view which is significantly different from traditional views of how learning language occurs.

It is a view of learning language which is based on two sets of assumptions. One set is related to how language needs to be organised if it is going to be optimally learned — that is, in wholes. The other set of assumptions relate to the very nature of learning itself. When these two sets of assumptions are brought together, a view of language learning results which goes something like this:

> All the linguistic and sociolinguistic systems and sub-systems need to be present. If young learners witness demonstrations of wholes of language being used and are constrained to engage with them they can, if they wish, focus on any of the sub-parts. They could, for example, focus on the phonemic and/ or graphic systems and perhaps learn something about the way those systems of the language work. Then again, they may need to attend to the syntax and add something from that to their burgeoning syntactic control. On the other hand, they may decide to hook into some aspect of the sociolinguistic rules associated with whatever is being demonstrated (see breakfast conversation example, page 34). Whatever they decide to focus on there needs to be enough information there for them to gain insights into how the system which we call language works, and how all the sub-systems which make it up work within it.

In other words, there needs to be sufficient information in the demonstration for the learner to be able to seek out and establish what Gregory Bateson has referred to as "the patterns which connect" *(Bateson, 1979)*. It is a **whole** language approach because the emphasis in on demonstrating **wholes** of language. The teacher creates contexts in which learners are presented with demonstrations of language to be learned which are wholes.

So what? Why is this important?

Isn't it just a matter of the teacher's predilection, of exercising a right of free choice, as it were? Isn't this just another of the endless method debates which have dogged literacy education for the last century?

The answer is, "No!"

It is important because once the decision is made to adopt the principle of presenting demonstrations of whole language as I've defined it, it sets in motion a whole chain of significant changes in the way things are done. This chain of events results in the setting up of learning contexts which are based on the conditions of learning described previously.

It is important because what results is based on a set of assumptions about learning, language and language learning which are really quite different from those to which most of us are accustomed.

It is important because this difference is a most difficult matter for many teachers, parent, the general public, and even learners themselves, to grasp. Many of us are so imbued with another view of learning that we take its tenets utterly for granted, so much so that we almost cannot comprehend the possibility that there might be other ways of thinking about how language forms are learned. When other ways are suggested we are inclined to shut our ears feeling that merely to listen to them is quite literally a heresy.

It is important because it is a view of learning and teaching which is not easily understood nor appreciated by those of us who have been imbued with another, more mechanistic, teacher-directed view of learning and teaching. This view advocates that learning is best achieved by simplifying what has to be learned through fragmentation of the total act.

The Alternative to the Theory of Whole Language: The Fragmentationist Theory of Learning Language

The alternative to the theoretical approach which I have labelled whole language, would be to peel off one of those layers of language depicted in Atwell's co-axial cable metaphor (see page ???) and attempt to teach a learner to control it while it is isolated from the other systems of language with which it is naturally associated when meanings are being constructed.

An example is the traditional grammar, phonics or spelling lesson. In the traditional grammar lesson the grammatical system is pulled free from the complex web of other linguistic systems (the meaning system, the phonemic system, the pragmatic system, etc.) and is taught as a system in its own right with its own integrity. The learner is presented with demonstrations of how grammar works in isolation from its role in shaping and moulding meaning. The subtle patterns which connect each of the linguistic systems that work cooperatively to produce intended meanings are thus broken. In the traditional phonics and/or spelling programme the graphophonic system is peeled away from the syntactic and semantic systems of language and the patterns which connect each to effective reading and/or writing are lost. The learner is left to work out what the patterns which connect are, in artificial and contrived ways which seriously complicate the process of learning. The majority find the task of orchestrating all the separate bits extremely complex.

The logic which lies behind a decision to fragment is based on the assumption that the task in its entirety is far too complex and needs to be simplified. Simplification equates with fragmentation. Once the decision to simplify is made, a whole chain of teaching-learning events is set in motion. For a start, the expectations are different: learners are expected to learn **all** that's in the demonstration; the responsibility (focus of control) shifts from learner to teacher; approximations are not accepted; responses are basically error hunts, and so on. In other words, the conditions of learning change significantly once the decision to fragment the demonstration is taken. A different learning context, and a different cognitive behaviour setting results.

Such a context is essentially one which complicates the learning process for the learner, because making sense becomes almost impossible. Learners who cannot make sense of the demonstrations being provided will soon cease to engage with them. Non-engagement with demonstrations is the sensible and predictable response to non-sense. Gregory Bateson recognised this situation when he wrote:

"Break the pattern which connects the items of learning and you necessarily destroy all quality." *(Bateson, 1979)*

This book has been about maximising the quality of literacy learning by helping teachers to understand how they can maintain the patterns which connect.

References

Atwell, M.A. *Reading, writing, speaking, listening: Language in response to context* in Hardt, V. (Ed) **Teaching Reading with the other Language Arts**, IRA, Delaware, 1983.

Bateson, G. **Mind and Nature; a necessary unity**, Wildwood House, Great Britain, 1979.

Birnbaum, J. & Emig, J. *Creating minds: Created texts: Writing and reading,* in Parker, R. & Davis, F. (Eds) **Developing Literacy: Young Children's Use of Language**, IRA, Delaware, 1983.

Brown, H. & Cambourne, B.L. **Read and Retell**, Sydney, Methuen, 1987.

Boomer, G. *Organising the nation for literacy.* Paper given at 13th Australian National Reading Conference, Sydney, 1987.

Bunbury R. *Books? A thing you only read at school,* reported in Sydney Morning Herald, 16 Aug. 1985.

Cambourne, B.L. *A naturalistic study of the language performance of grade 1 rural and urban schoolchildren.* Unpublished doctoral thesis, James Cook University of North Queensland, 1972.

Cambourne, B.L. *Organising the profession for literacy,* Paper given at 13th Australian National Reading Conference, Sydney, 1987.

Cambourne, B.L. *A sure-fire, never-fail, K-12 recipe for producing a-literate, dependent learners,* in Comber/Hancock (Eds) **Independent Learners**. ARA, Adelaide, 1987.

Chomsky, C. *Language Development after Six.* **HGSEA Bulletin** XIV, No 3. Spring 1970 (pp.14-16).

Curtiss, S. **Genie: A Psycholinguistic Study of a Modern Day Wild Child**, Academic Press, New York, 1977.

Hughes, T. *Foreword:* **Children as Writers 2**, Heinemann, London, 1975.

Iredell, H. *Eleanor learns to read,* Education, No. 19, (pp 233-238), 1898.

Jaynes, J. **The Origins of Consciousness in the Breakdown of the Bicamersal Mind**, Houghton Mifflin, Boston, 1976.

Johnson, T. & Louis, D. **Literacy through Literature**, Methuen, Sydney, 1985.

Koestler, A. **The Ghost in the Machine**, Picador, London, 1975.

Logan, N. & Cambourne, B.L. *South Coast Reading Evaluation Study,* South Coast Region of Education, 1983.

Martin, J. & Rothery, J. *Writing Project Report No. 1,* Department of Linguistics, University of Sydney, 1980.

Moffet, J. **Teaching the Universe of Discourse**, Houghton Mifflin, Boston, 1968.

Protherough, R. **Encouraging Writing**, Methuen, London, 1983.

Rousch, P.D. & Cambourne, B.L. *A psycholinguistic study of the reading processes of proficient, average and low ability readers, grades 2-8,* Riverina College of Advanced Education, 1978.

Scollan, R. *Plenary address,* National Reading Conference, Tampa, 1987.

Smith, F. *Demonstrations, engagement, and sensitivity: A revised approach to language learning,* **Language Arts**, 1981.

Smith, F. **Writing and the Writer**, Heinemann, London, 1982.

Warner, E. *Do we understand sentences from the outside in or the inside out?* **Daedalus,** Summer, 1973 (pp 185-194).

Williams, P. *The avid and non-avid reader: A descriptive study of the silent reading behaviour of readers who can and do and can and won't* in Bessell-Brown, et al (Eds) **Reading in the '80s,** Australian Reading Association, Adelaide, 1980 (pp 49-80).

Weir, R. **Language in the Crib**, Mouton and Co., The Hague, 1962.

Acknowledgements

Although I accept full responsibility for the contents of this book, it will be obvious that it was not a sole effort. It owes much to many people, including:

* Hazel Brown, my co-researcher. She gave me the privilege of working in her classroom as she turned some tenuous theory I had developed into workable classroom practice.

* The children who were members of Hazel Brown's class 1985–1988. They were very astute co-researchers who kept both of us on course.

* The principal of Balarang Primary School, Max Green, and his staff. I was always made to feel welcome.

* My academic colleague, Jan Turbill. She is one of the most efficient crap-detectors I've met. Much of the final shape of this book is a consequence of the many hours she spent reacting to the ideas in it.

* Ken Goodman, Yetta Goodman, Don Graves, Don Holdaway, Frank Smith, Jerry Harste, Peter Rousch. Many of the ideas in this book are based on what they've taught me.

* My editors, Libby Handy and Penny Scown, for their support and the subtle way they kept me on course.

Finally, I am forever indebted to Olwyn Cambourne and our children. They gave me a very special kind of support while this book was being written.

Brian Cambourne

Wollongong, September 1988.